ENDORSEMENTS

Tim and his daughter, Rachel, could not have written a more timely message for those praying for prodigals. There is heavenly wisdom in these pages, coupled with faith-filled intercession that will in no doubt allow you to trust and rest in the promises of God. I couldn't help but rejoice already—for the prodigals who will be coming home.

Kathy Troccoli
Singer, Songwriter, Author

As I was reading over the chapter titles of this new book by Tim Sheets and his daughter, Rachel, I felt that this book will impact the hearts of people in a powerful way. The points in each chapter that are being brought out will help guide us to have a more powerful, positive focus that will help establish a confidence that the prodigals are coming home. Each chapter sends out a powerful message of finding identity and hope that unlocks destiny for those who are lost. The point of restored purpose truly ignites our understanding that there is more for each of us and helps lay a foundation that reveals what we have in our relationship with the Father and others. I encourage you to be ready to see the restoration of our loved ones as we see the prodigals coming into their original intended purpose and identity. The prayers and decrees in this book will help set a focus and foundation to stand on to see those who are lost come home and find their identity in Him. This book also gives great insight and strategy in how to stand in, and on, the promises of the Lord and see the prodigals come home and find their God-given destiny.

Pat McManus
Kingdom Impact Center Aurora

It is my absolute honor to endorse this amazing book, *Come Home*, written by my friends, Apostle Tim Sheets and his daughter, Rachel Shafer. This book is a strategic manual that gives the body of Christ much-needed clarity concerning the power of prayer and decrees. Within these pages are testimonies, decrees, and insights that will encourage and assist believers to work together with the Lord in prayer as He brings about the fulfillment of His prophetic promise of reaping the "billion soul harvest." This book is a call to the wall of intercession, and it's a valuable resource of information that will help equip each reader with a greater understanding and resolve to unrelentingly stand on that wall and refuse to back down until we see the prodigals come home! Thank you, Apostle Tim and Rachel, for your diligence in prayer and research and for your commitment and willingness to write this very insightful and timely book.

Gina Gholston
Author of Awakening the Church to Awaken a Nation, Dreams of Awakening, and *Carry On*

Within the pages of this book by Pastor Tim and Rachel lies the current heartbeat of our Father God—He wants His family back. This is Heaven's revelation in real time about Christ and His church releasing power into broken lives, to recover past seasons and restore the prodigal to whom they were originally intended to be. *Come Home* is a call to the church to come back to the center of the Gospel. Yet not in an introverted revivalism, but a true partnering with Heaven, decreeing His Word to see a massive harvest of souls come home.

Reverend Jen Tringale
Author, Speaker, and Podcast Host

In a world where hearts ache and spirits yearn for the return of their prodigals, *Come Home* emerges as a beacon of hope and a source of spiritual sustenance. This remarkable book, birthed from a divine calling and nurtured with fervent prayers, delivers a message of unwavering faith and profound insight. In these pages, authors Tim Sheets and Rachel Shafer usher us into a realm of understanding, empowerment, and transformative grace. With a compassionate touch, they explore the journey of prodigals, shedding light on the profound role they are destined to play in the forthcoming billion-soul harvest. Through their teachings, they unveil the power of decrees, a spiritual practice that has the potential to shift destinies and transform lives. As you embark on the journey through *Come Home,* prepare to be inspired, equipped, and uplifted. Whether you're new to the practice of decreeing or a seasoned intercessor, this book offers something invaluable—a road map to guiding prodigals back into the loving embrace of their heavenly Father.

In a world where uncertainty can cast shadows over our faith, *Come Home* shines as a radiant source of light, guiding us all toward the promise of restoration and redemption. *Come Home* is not just a book, it's a companion for the journey of faith, a source of encouragement in times of doubt, and a beacon of hope for all those who believe in the power of prayer and the unwavering love of a heavenly Father. Endorse this book with your heart, and let its wisdom resonate within you. *Come Home* will undoubtedly become a cherished guide on your path to seeing the fulfillment of God's promises in the lives of those you hold dear.

Dr. Scott Reece
River City Church, Quad Cities

This book is a Kingdom book, a much-needed Kingdom book. My friends Tim Sheets and his daughter Rachel Shafer's new masterful work, *Come Home*, will revolutionize how you think, speak, pray, decree, and live regarding your prodigal. Tim and Rachel are gifted authors and teachers of the Word of God. Their writing style demonstrates their passionate teaching style in every book they've written together. After reading *Come Home*, you will agree that the revelation and empowerment held within these pages have the potential to wreck your life (for the good), redeem your lost loved ones, and position them to live where they were created to live, in His presence! *Come Home* should be on the bookshelf of everyone with a lost son or daughter. Among other things, this powerful new book is a road map for retrieving, empowering, and releasing this present-day prodigal generation into their purpose. You will learn of our partnership with angels and what role we play together in this process of bringing in the Great Harvest. Thank you, Tim and Rachel, for writing this book. There will be many testimonies of redemption and restoration from this work. Acts 16:31-32 says: *"They answered, 'Believe in the Lord Jesus, and you will be saved—you and all your family.' Then they prophesied the word of the Lord over him and all his family."*

Dr. Greg Hood, ThD
President, Kingdom University
Apostolic Leader, The Network of Five-Fold Ministers and Churches, and Kingdom Life Ekklesia, Franklin, Tennessee
Author of *The Gospel of the Kingdom, Sonship According to the Kingdom, Citizenship According to the Kingdom*, and *Rebuilding the Broken Altar—Awaking Out of Chaos*
www.GregHood.org

COME HOME

PRAY, PROPHESY, &
PROCLAIM GOD'S
PROMISES OVER
YOUR PRODIGAL

COME
HOME

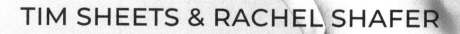

TIM SHEETS & RACHEL SHAFER

DESTINY IMAGE® PUBLISHERS, INC.
P.O. Box 310, Shippensburg, PA 17257-0310

"Publishing cutting-edge prophetic resources to supernaturally empower the body of Christ"

This book and all other Destiny Image and Destiny Image Fiction books are available at Christian bookstores and distributors worldwide.

For more information on foreign distributors, call 717-532-3040.

Reach us on the Internet: www.destinyimage.com.

ISBN 13 TP: 978-0-7684-7759-7

ISBN 13 eBook: 978-0-7684-7760-3

For Worldwide Distribution, Printed in the U.S.A.

2 3 4 5 6 7 8 / 28 27 26 25 24

DEDICATION

We dedicate this book to all those who are praying or
have prayed for a prodigal to come home. God sees.
He knows their names. Thank you for never giving up
and we are believing with you for an amazing harvest
of prodigals, including yours.

ACKNOWLEDGMENTS

Thank you Destiny Image and Larry Sparks for your belief and support of what we do. We are blessed to have the relationship we have with you and appreciate your encouragement and input.

We acknowledge those who have paved the way, gone before us, prayed us on, and encouraged us.

Our amazing book team—Katelyn Cundiff, Marie Fox, and Carol Sheets—for the multiplied hours of helping the vision of this book become reality, we thank you. Words are not enough but we pray you know how valued you are to the process.

To each one of you, both in person and online, we appreciate you so very much for all the prayers and encouragement and your faithfulness to the assignments God gives us to implement. We couldn't do it without you, nor would we want to. Thank you.

Most importantly, we thank our Father. He invites us all to *Come Home*.

Thus says the Lord, "Restrain your voice from weeping and your eyes from tears, for your work [raising of your children, prayer] *will be rewarded," says the Lord; "and your children will return from the enemy's land. There is [confident] hope for your future," says the Lord; "Your children will come back to their own country."*

—JEREMIAH 31:16-17 AMP

CONTENTS

CONTENTS

FOREWORD

Apostle Tim Sheets and his daughter, Rachel Shafer, have provided an absolutely essential go-to-guide for praying your prodigal child back home. I write these words from a unique perspective; I was interviewing Apostle Tim about one topic and our conversation took a strange turn.

We were talking about angel armies and revival, but there was such a sovereign grace and strong anointing as he began to share about God's heart for prodigals coming home and that in this new era of revival, we would witness an unprecedented turnaround when it comes to lost family members—*especially sons and daughters*—being supernaturally awakened to return to their first love.

Coupled with the engaging writing, revelation, and amazing mother's heart of Tim's daughter, Rachel, this book is unlike anything I've seen. It has powerful prayers and decrees that equip you to storm Heaven for your lost children. It has a strong, encouraging prophetic perspective that gives you the big picture of *why* God is emphasizing this supernatural *prodigal-come-home* campaign. And it links your child coming back to Jesus to their identity, purpose, and assignment being fulfilled in the great reformation that is here and now.

Your son and daughter was saved by the blood of Jesus, not to simply sit in a pew, but to be a reformer who overthrows the powers of darkness in culture. Hell trembles at what this book is going to unleash into the world—the flash floods of Heaven being released by prodigals that were prayed back home!

Larry Sparks, MDiv
Publisher, Destiny Image
Author of *Pentecostal Fire* and *The Fire That Never Sleeps*
larrysparksministries.com

PREFACE

It has been prophesied that a "billion soul harvest" is coming. It is our belief that prodigals will be included in that number, and within them are destinies that will be stirred up and released, with lives being changed because of their return to the Father's House.

One often thinks of a prodigal as a son or daughter, but perhaps your prodigal is a spouse, a relative or friend. Anyone who has walked away from what they know to be spiritually true can be considered a prodigal. In the parable of the prodigal son in the Bible, the man's son recklessly and wastefully spends his inheritance. In our current time, we think of this as someone choosing a worldly lifestyle, indulging in every desire and wasting their purpose and destiny. In the context of the parable, the prodigal son also means someone who is a sinner, one who is spiritually lost, and someone who has returned to family and faith after an absence.

An incredible aspect of this parable is the extravagant, lavish grace given by a father to his returning son. We can know and understand from this story, the power of the great love God has for all and how He longs to welcome them home.

Recently, God has emphasized to us His heart for the coming generation. We have wept over them, prayed over them, fasted for them. It has seemed urgent to us in our spirit that the time is now. These have been encouraging words as so many have been praying for the return of their loved ones to His embrace. Some have been captured and captivated by the current culture, trapped by the forever loser into lives they were never meant to live. Families have been contending for loved ones to return to Him. Sometimes in the midst of the battle, the war, hearts and hope become disillusioned and despair tries to overwhelm our faith. *We must not lose heart.*

Our prayer is that within the pages of this book you will find resources and ministry to help you continue to stand. We have included messages, decrees, and prayers, and we join our faith with yours to call your prodigal home. There are words within these pages that will build you up as well. We do not lose heart, we stand strong. We have angel armies' assistance and even when we can't see it, He's working.

Be encouraged.

But God!

Tim Sheets and **Rachel Shafer**

INTRODUCTION

O ur prayer for this book is to equip the reader to boldly make a stand for the prodigals who may be in your lives, whether a relative, friend, acquaintance, or someone God lays upon your heart. We know that prodigals will be a huge part of awakening and reformation and that His desire is to bring them home and restore to them their purpose.

Upon these pages you will find God's Word, Prophetic Words, Decrees, Prayers, Testimonies, Teaching, and more to strengthen you, encourage you, and assure you that He will save your children. You will understand how to activate angel armies to assist in bringing your prodigal home. You can expect a refreshed anointing to press in and press on as you take back what the enemy has tried to steal. We have God's promise.

HOW (AND WHY) TO DECREE

It is important for us to understand decrees: what they are, why we use them, and how to apply them as part of our prayer assignments. At the end of each chapter in this book, we have suggested decrees for you, and so we are providing the following information, copied in part from my book, *Planting the Heavens—Releasing the Authority of the Kingdom Through Your Words, Prayers, and Declarations.* If you would like to know more about making decrees, you can order the book at TimSheets.org.

Decrees are word seeds. Psalm 103:20 says that angels hearken to the voice of God's Word. The words we speak give angels something to work with, and it is important to understand just how powerful our words are.

Job 22:28 (KJV) says, *"Thou shalt also **decree** a thing, and it shall be established unto thee: and the light shall shine upon thy ways."* The NKJV says it this way, *"You will also **declare** a thing, and it will be established...."* This is why you will hear *decree* and *declare* interchanged a lot.

DECREE MEANS

When we decree, we are simply stating our prayer for a situation or person by saying emphatically what we are believing for that lines up with God's Word. We are, in essence, planting the heavens, seeding the atmosphere with His Word and our faith.

Isaiah 51:16 (NKJV) says, *"And I have put My words in your mouth; I have covered you with the shadow of My hand, that I may plant the heavens, lay the foundations of the earth, and say to Zion, 'You are My people.'"*

This verse emphasizes that words are seeds—word seed decrees. This also includes prayer because prayers are words of communication seeded into the heavens and into the earth. Prayer is speech to God making a request, but it is also, at times, a decree of God's promises. Prayers express confidence in God's answering abilities, or they may ask for divine intervention into a situation.

The mouth (*peh*) is the opening of the body to sound forth God's words as seeds that grow to fullness until they are manifested in the heavens or in the earth (Strong's 6310). Our enemy, the forever loser, wants us to keep our mouths closed and is always seeking to silence Christ's body. But from the very beginning, God's original intent was for His sons and daughters to open their mouths and declare His words. He has put His Word in your mouth so that you will decree it and He can plant it into the atmosphere. The word *plant* is the Hebrew word *nata,* which means to plant, to fix, or to set in place (Strong's 5193). God Himself was the original Gardener, and we have inherited that job from Him as His heirs.

We have to understand the power in our decrees of God's Word. We have this promise: when we stand in faith and decree what God says, when we refuse to back off, when we refuse to abandon that word seed, when we water the seed with our faith, our prayers, our praise, our confession, and our steadfast trust, the seed will produce after its kind.

Never give up on a seed you plant. Never give up on God's Word. Never. Don't negate it. We are supposed to make decrees that break loose hell's grip. We should expect God's word seeds that we decree to produce after their kind, the word of promise to come to pass, no matter what it is, and the word seeds we sow to become fruitful and multiply.

I hope this helps give some understanding as to why we decree. I encourage you to be bold and speak the decrees in this book, and add your own, out loud and with confidence, knowing

God backs His Word and it does not return void. Give the angels something to work with!

1

RESTORING LOST PURPOSE

> *Thus says the Lord: "Restrain your voice from weeping and your eyes from tears, for your work [raising of your children, prayer] will be rewarded," says the Lord; "and your children will return from the enemy's land. There is [confident] hope for your future," says the Lord; "Your children will come back to their own country"* **(Jeremiah 31:16-17 AMP).**

Many are standing on God's Word and His promises regarding the return of prodigals, whether it be their own child or loved one, a friend, or those contending for a wave of revival that includes the lost returning home. In the study and preparation for this book, we came across a powerful truth regarding the biblical illustration of the Prodigal Son story. This word prepares the foundation regarding what we have thought was lost purpose, but God's plan always contains redemption, as the following paragraphs illustrate.

Luke 15:20 (NKJV) says, concerning the prodigal son, *"...when he was still a great way off, his father...had compassion, and ran and fell on his neck and kissed him."*

Jewish history enlightens us as to why the father ran, and it is a stunning revelation. This man's son had demanded his inheritance, wanting what he considered to be his now, rather than when his father died, as was the custom of the day. After receiving his portion, the son left his home, turning his back on the values he had been taught. He eventually lost everything, wasting it all on parties and prostitutes, and ended up working in a pigpen. The son broke his father's heart, as well as breaking all the rules of the tight-knit community he had been brought up in. After he came to his senses, the son decided to return home. Luke 15:20 tells us his father saw his son when he was still a long way off and ran to him.

In those times, a Middle Eastern man never ran, because in order to do so he would have to raise up his tunic so he wouldn't trip, and in so doing would expose his bare legs. In that culture, it was considered humiliating and shameful for a man to show his bare legs. In addition, it was known that if a Jewish son lost his inheritance among Gentiles, and then returned home, the community would perform a ceremony called the *kezazah,* or a "ceremony of shame."

During this ceremony, they would break a large pot or pitcher in front of the son. As they smashed it into pieces, they would declare him to be cut off from his people, all ties broken, and he would no longer be welcome in the community.

This, then, brings us to the question: why did the father run to his son, which also brought a level of shame to himself? In essence, the father was running to get to his son in order to extend grace before anyone else could get to him with the law. He wanted to extend love, acceptance, welcome, and hope before anyone else could take it away. He wanted his son welcomed, not shamed with humiliation and rejection.

As onlookers watched the father run toward his son, reuniting, hugging and kissing him, it would be apparent there would be no *kezazah.* Instead, there would be a homecoming party, a celebration of his restoration, which only the father could bring. No rejection—his father bore the shame and showed everyone that his son was welcomed home.

The application for us is fairly obvious. Our Father bore our sin and shame through Jesus. We can be forgiven and redeemed, and even our lost purpose and destiny can be restored. As we repent, He wipes the slate clean and gives us a fresh start.

God's Promise: What He did for the prodigal son, He will do for you, and He will also do it for those for whom you are praying. Lost purpose will be recovered.

PURPOSE

The apostle Paul was a man of great purpose who understood destiny. In 2 Timothy, he wrote to his son in the faith, Timothy, concerning the subject.

> *For God saved us and called us to live a holy life. He did this, not because we deserved it, but because that was his plan from before the beginning of time—to show us his grace through Christ Jesus.*
> **(2 Timothy 1:9 NLT)**

> *Who has saved us and called us with a holy calling, not according to our works, but according to His own purpose and grace which was given to us in Christ Jesus before time began.*
> **(2 Timothy 1:9 NKJV)**

The word *purpose* is the Greek word *prothesis* (Strong's 4286).[1] *Pro* is before. *Prothesis* means to set before, to set up, an exposition, and it also means to resolve or design.

You can easily recognize two English words derived from *prothesis*. First of all is the word *thesis*, which is a written report. An English teacher may have asked you to write a thesis on a particular subject or topic in school. *Thesis* can also refer to an essay or written composition concerning a specific viewpoint. In some situations, it could refer to a book.

Paul said to Timothy, and to you and I today: God wrote a thesis on you and recorded it in a book He has in Heaven. Before you ever entered the womb, God wrote His thesis on the details involving the design of your purpose, listing the intentions and paths He had in mind for you.

In eternity past, there came a time when God, the Creator of Heaven and earth, sat down and studied your life and what it would mean, why it would be, and then He composed a "written thesis" entitled *Purpose*. Amazingly, your life has spent time in God's mind.

One such thesis would be titled "Tim's Purpose," in which He began to write a composition on my particular purpose. When He finished the book, He said, "Now, when the time is right, I will create him."

Other theses would be titled Tom's Purpose, or Dave's Purpose, or Rachel's Purpose. And one has *your* name on it. God sat down, wrote a thesis about you and recorded it in Heaven. He said, "When the time is right, I'll create him or her." Which means the time must be right, because you're here!

The time is "right" for you to understand and fulfill your destiny. The time is "right" for you to begin to live out the thesis of God for your life. Your being alive now is proof of it. Just as God took a book called the Bible and quickened it, making it a *rhema* (living) word to us, so He can, and will, do with the book concerning you.

God wants to "quicken His thesis" about you *to* you. He wants His words of purpose made alive inside you. He wants it to become *rhema*. He wants His composition written about you to come alive so that His book about you isn't just read—it's lived. It's a living thesis for you, residing inside you. Make no mistake about it. God, the Author, wrote your plan well. He left out no details. He thought through all of the chapters and, as Paul would write to the Hebrews, God is not only the Author, He's also the Finisher.

He will help you finish the journey. He will assist you in finishing the "plans." He will help you on all that is set forth. God says, "I wrote it down. I made it plain. I declared your purpose and I'll even help you do it!"

Prothesis—before you were born God wrote your thesis. Then He made you with everything it would take to do it. With His Holy Spirit quickening and guiding, and with His help, you can do it.

I want us to see this word in connection with another word.

> *For [the] administration of the fulness of times; to head up all things in the Christ, the things in the heavens and the things upon the earth; in him, in whom we have also obtained an inheritance, being marked out beforehand according to the purpose of him who works all things according to the counsel of his own will.*
>
> **(Ephesians 1:10-11 Darby)**

Purpose is the Greek word *prothesis*. Counsel is the Greek word *boulē* (Strong's 1012) and it means the will, to decree, to aim, and it also refers to the decision-making process of government. The parliamentary government in modern Greece is called the *boulē*, not the Congress like in the United States.

Why do they use the word *boulē*? Because *boulē* means deliberation and reflection. The Greek government reflects and deliberates before the decrees are made. They reflect on the projects needed as they meet in counsel together. They reflect and deliberate before the will is written down (before it's recorded).

God says before *We* made you (God said in Genesis, let *Us* make man in Our image and likeness, referring to the Godhead of Father, Son, and Holy Spirit), before *We* wrote your thesis, We reflected on your purpose. We deliberated and thought it through. We exchanged ideas concerning you and took counsel together concerning Our will for your life.

The ways intended for you were reflected upon by the parliament of Heaven. The parliamentary counsel of Heaven decreed and declared the intended purpose for each man and woman. As They wrote the thesis for each person, They had it recorded, and when it was the right time, we were born.

David says in Psalm 139, *"My days were written down before there was one of them."* Acts 13:36 (NKJV) says, *"For David, after he served his own generation by the will of God, fell asleep, was buried with his fathers...."* The word *will* in that verse is *boulē*. The parliamentary counsel of Heaven had a purpose, a thesis, for David to accomplish and David served it. Acts 13:36 (AMPC) says, *"For David, after he had served God's will and purpose and counsel in his own generation, fell asleep [in death]...."*

David discovered and fulfilled the purpose of God for his life. He had purpose in his generation and he accomplished it. You, too, have purpose. God wrote your story beforehand and is now working on paths that will enable you to fulfill it in your generation.

I said earlier there were two words readily seen in the Greek word for purpose (*prothesis*). One is, of course, *thesis*. The second word is *prosthesis*, which refers to artificial limbs. It used to be if someone's leg had to be cut off, a wooden leg or a peg was put in its place. Why make an artificial limb? To restore a lost purpose. To restore lost movement and balance and to restore some kind of use or purpose that was missing, cut off.

What a word this is for us! What a hope this gives us. You may say, "My life has been cut off from any real meaning. There's something missing. Years ago, I did this or that and I feel cut off because of it. I sinned. I did something I'm ashamed of. I did something I know was absolutely wrong. I miserably failed. I made decisions that were selfish. I made choices that were directly opposed to why I'm here."

Quite possibly, a situation may have occurred that you had no control over and cut you off. Perhaps a tragedy took place, or you experienced a broken relationship, or suffered some form of abuse. Because of that, it seems as if you've been severed from any real purpose. You've been cut off from a life of significance and meaning and the balance in your life was thrown askew.

God may have a thesis that He reflected upon and wrote for you, but life or fate has written you a different one and you're living cut off from God's thesis. You can't complete His thesis for you because what is needed to do so was amputated from you. What I want to emphasize is that your purpose—the reason you are here—doesn't change. It never changes. God is not rewriting your story; He already wrote it!

Because He is God and is all-powerful and all-knowing, if you will turn to Him, trust Him, and let Him, then He, the Master Surgeon, can reconstruct lost purpose. Prosthesis: He can give you a new limb. He can give you what it takes to restore lost movement, lost balance, and lost purpose, even if it was amputated from you.

You say, "But, Apostle Tim, I would walk with a limp." So did Jacob! That lying, stealing, conniving, cheating man who wrestled with God went on to fulfill his purpose and destiny. He wrestled with his destiny for 97 years, but he finally got it. Yes, he walked with a limp, but he walked and God's thesis was reconstructed with, eventually, the Messiah coming through his descendants. When submitted to God, Jacob's purpose was reconstructed.

You may say or be thinking, "Well, where my purpose is concerned, I just don't have a leg to stand on." God says, "I'll make one for you because My purpose is not changeable." God says, "Me and you—we can do it. I'll help you. I'll do miracles. I'll help you fulfill My words."

Hebrews 6:17-19 (KJV) says concerning this:

> *Wherein God, willing more abundantly to show unto the heirs of promise the immutability of his counsel, confirmed it by an oath: that by two immutable things, in which it was impossible for God to lie, we might have a strong consolation, who have fled for refuge to lay hold upon the hope set before us: which hope we have as an anchor of the soul, both sure and stedfast, and which entereth into that within the veil.*

Immutability and immutable mean unchangeable. It's the Greek word *ametathetos* derived from *metatithemi* (Strong's 276/3346). The theme is unchangeable! The theme of my *boulē* is unchangeable. *Metatithemi!*

Let's use a word we may understand better for immutable: the word *mutations*. No mutations! God says, "No mutations. My theme is set before you. It's like concrete. No mutations." God says, "Let that give you strong consolation. Let that be an anchor for your soul." God says, "My theme, My thesis, My purpose is set before you. And if cut off, I will restore it." He confirms it with an oath!

He says, "I, God, do solemnly swear that you can be who I have made you to be. I, God, do solemnly swear that you are an heir to My promises for your life. I swear I can reconstruct you. I swear My future for you is good. I swear there's hope before you. I swear I have a plan for you. I swear I have given you a destiny. I swear My thesis was thought through about you. And I swear that before you were ever born, I saw to it that you would have all you would need, along with My help, to accomplish it."

God says, "I promise all My promises to you are good ones. I'll do what I said. Just walk together with Me. Walk in relationship with Me and you will discover and live out a life filled with purpose, significance, and meaning."

WRESTLING WITH DESTINY

But Jacob stayed behind by himself, and a man wrestled with him until daybreak. When the man saw that he couldn't get the best of Jacob as they wrestled, he deliberately threw Jacob's hip out of joint. The man said, "Let me go; it's daybreak." Jacob said, "I'm not letting you go 'til you bless me." The man said, "What's your name?" He answered, "Jacob." The man said, "But no longer. Your name is no longer Jacob. From now on it's Israel (God-Wrestler); you've wrestled with God and you've come through." Jacob asked, "And what's your name?" The man said, "Why do you want to know my name?" And then, right then and there, he blessed him. Jacob named the place Peniel (God's Face) because, he said, "I saw God face-to-face and lived to tell the story!" The sun came up as he left Peniel, limping because of his hip. (This is why Israelites to this day don't eat the hip muscle; because Jacob's hip was thrown out of joint.)

(Genesis 32:24-31 MSG)

These verses occur when Jacob is 97 years old. It is the fascinating story of a prodigal wrestling with God concerning his destiny until the break of day. The name *Jacob* means supplanter, deceiver, conniver, cheater, defrauder, manipulator, the liar.

For 97 years, Jacob had lived up to the name Isaac and Rebekah had given him. He was a man of selfish ambitions and goals and he preyed upon the weaknesses of others. An example of this was when Jacob refused to feed his brother, Esau, until Esau sold him his birthright. He took advantage of his brother's weaknesses to promote himself. Whatever it took to get his way was fine with him.

Jacob was a loner. He liked being alone and didn't need anyone. People were simply tools he used to advance his agenda. Family meant very little to Jacob. He had tricked his father into giving him Esau's birthright, which had destroyed his relationship with his brother. He couldn't care less about building a family. In fact, he stayed a bachelor until he was 77 years old. Jacob didn't know how to love someone else.

Amazingly, how Jacob had become didn't change God's purpose and destiny for his life. Before the foundation of the world, before there was one day to Jacob's life, God sat down and wrote his thesis, his purpose for being. God said, "I need someone who will help Me start a nation of people—a nation I will be with and will bless. One that I will call *Israel*. Jacob is the man I choose for this. I'll change his name to Israel and work on him until I draw out My purpose in his life. Jacob is the man for the job. That is his thesis, his destiny, and his purpose."

Though Jacob had taken wrong paths, as prodigals so often do, God continued the process of bringing forth his destiny. When Jacob was 77 years old, Isaac said to him, "That's it, Jacob. You've lived at home long enough. Now go to Padanaram and find a wife." And Jacob did. In fact, he found two wives: Rachel and Leah.

On Jacob's way to Padanaram, he came to a certain spot and stopped for the night. He didn't realize it was the destiny spot at first and wouldn't realize it for years. He piled up some rocks for his pillow and went to sleep. While asleep, God appeared to him in a dream.

Jacob saw Heaven open and the angels of God were ascending and descending on a ladder. God appeared to him and said, "I am the God of Abraham and Isaac and I want to give to you the land you're walking on. Your seed shall be like the dust of the earth. I'll be with you and keep you."

Genesis 28:15 tells us in essence that God said, "I will not leave you until I have done what I have spoken to you. I'm not going to leave you alone because My thesis on you is not changeable. I will not leave you until I do what I told you I would do." Jacob woke up and named that spot *Bethel,* which means the house of God, the gate of Heaven.

Rachel and Leah are stories of purpose in their own right. When Jacob arrived at Padanaram, he saw Rachel and his eyes lit up. She was beautiful. After a time, he asked Laban, her father, if he could marry her and it was agreed upon. Jacob worked for seven years for Rachel, but on their wedding night, Laban had tricked the trickster. He snuck Leah into the wedding tent in the darkness, instead of Rachel.

Leah was the opposite of Rachel. She was not pretty. She was extremely nearsighted and considered as not desirable. No one wanted to marry her. Knowing this, her father decided to do something, which is why he snuck her into the tent. When Jacob woke up the next morning, he could see clearly what had happened, saying to Laban, "What have you done?"

But again, God had a purpose in mind. God saw something in Leah that no one else could see. By man's standards, Leah was unattractive, but God saw a girl of great worth. He saw purpose and destiny.

What did God see in Leah? He saw Gad, Asher, Reuben, Simeon, Levi, Judah, Issachar, and Zebulun—eight of the 12 tribes of Israel. God saw ongoing heritage to this day. God always seeks to draw out purpose.

After living 20 years in Padanaram, God said, "Jacob, I want you to return to Bethel. I want you to go back home. I want you to go back to the place that you named the house of God."

Jacob didn't want to go. Why? Because he would have to face his brother Esau, the one he had deceived, connived against, and hurt. The one he manipulated, bruised and used. Jacob was convinced that Esau, a great hunter, would kill him. *If I go back, I'm dead,* he thought.

Jacob was convinced Esau would kill him, his wives and all his children. But the call of God was strong upon Jacob at this point. Destiny's currents were drawing him, and Jacob decided to start for home, bringing all of his family with him.

Genesis 32 occurs the night before Jacob is going to see Esau for the first time in 20 years. Tomorrow would be the day. Jacob had sent his men ahead to tell Esau he was coming. With these men, he had sent hundreds of animals as presents for Esau. He sent flock after flock, herd after herd, waves of presents for his brother. He was hoping it would appease Esau's wrath. *Maybe if I give him cattle, sheep, and camels, He won't kill me and my family,* Jacob thought.

After Jacob sent his men with all of the animals, Jacob sent his wife and children across the stream Jabbok, which left him alone. Wrestling with your destiny can sometimes be a very lonely thing. As he was there alone, the night wore on, and a man appeared in Jacob's camp. We know today it wasn't an ordinary man. God was coming to Jacob in bodily form.

Jacob was seeing God again like he had seen him 20 years ago at Bethel, at the house of God. He had come back and heard God again. While Jacob had changed some things, he hadn't changed nearly enough. He was still the great manipulator, the cheater. As incredible as it seems to us today, when Jacob sees the Lord coming into his camp, he dives at Him and starts to wrestle Him. He grabs hold and will not let go.

For a very good reason, God lets Jacob do it. Can you picture Jacob holding onto God's leg and being dragged around the camp? God allowed that to take place. What's going on here? We have to see under the skin of this a bit. Just who is Jacob wrestling with? We know that, physically, it was God, but who was he really wrestling with? He was wrestling with himself. He was fighting with himself because when God's presence comes to an individual's life, to a prodigal's life, there's an exposing of flesh, attitudes, desires, sin, and heart motives. After 97 years, it had all come to a head. Jacob is confronted with who he is, and what he's become, and he doesn't like it.

Jacob knows that what he did was wrong. He knows he cheated to get what he has, by manipulating and using people to get what he wants. He knows his actions and words hurt so many. He knows he lived a life of greed and selfishness. He has been vengeful and self-aspiring, treating people and family with no respect. He stepped on everyone he could to advance himself.

Jacob is now confronted with the fact that is who he is. In sheer frustration he lashes out at God, and God lets him do it. It's almost as though God was saying, "It's okay, Jacob. Go ahead and get it out of you. Use Me this time because I can take it. You don't have to use others. Use Me. Go ahead and get it out because it's stopping your destiny. Purge yourself of it once and for all."

Jacob, having come to grips with who he was, grabs hold of God and says, "You have to change me. I want to be a person You can bless. I want to know why I'm here. I have to know Your plan for my life and the thesis You wrote about me. God, help me. God, bless me."

When God knew the repentance was real, He then knocked Jacob's hip out of joint and from that day forward Jacob walked with a limp. It would remind him every day, "You ran from God for 97 years. Don't do it again. Walk with the Lord and in His ways."

God then says to him, "What is your name?" And Jacob probably hung his head as he said, "Jacob. My name is cheater, manipulator, deceiver." He probably felt the shame that accompanied his ways. But God was ready now to bring forth Jacob's destiny and God said to him, "You will no longer be called Jacob. From now on your name is Israel. Israel means Prince of God. From now on you are a Prince of God."

The thesis written before there was one day to Jacob's life was finally brought about. Jacob began as a new man to walk out his purpose. He was Israel, not Jacob. He was a Prince of God, not a deceiver. The unfolding of purpose transformed him and he became a completely different man. He thought differently, talked differently. He became very devoted to his family and actually became a loving and kind man.

Prodigals often wrestle with who they are or who they have become. Sometimes they wrestle with God, fighting Him because of things that have happened—things they feel He should have changed or stopped. A prodigal will wrestle with conscience, motives of the heart, selfishness, pride, and greed. They may wonder why they are here, and what their destiny and purpose is.

But the great Father of love and compassion says to the prodigals, as He said to Jacob, "I am not leaving you alone until what I have declared over you takes place. I will wrestle destiny out of you. I will wrestle with you until the purpose I have in mind for you comes to pass. I will not give up on you until My destiny, planned before you were ever born, comes to pass."

A TESTIMONY (ANONYMOUS)

The amount of sadness I feel when I look back on my childhood is numbing. I know there are many who have gone through far worse, but I also know I didn't deserve to be sexually assaulted at the age of six by a cousin. I didn't deserve to be beaten for opening a bag of potato chips when there was already one open.

No child deserves to be lied to, belittled, abused, and brokenhearted.

I grew up in church and I've been saved since I was five years old. Though I made mistakes and failed Him many times, He never forsook me, and His mercies have been new every morning. I sometimes have to remind myself we all have stumbled, but it's all about the comeback.

I was in a bad relationship for several years following high school that caused serious damage. While everything seemed fine in the beginning, it slowly began to change, and this person cheated on me, he lied to me constantly, told me how stupid I was, called me every name in the book, told me that I needed to kill myself, and physically, emotionally, and mentally abused me. The amount of lies I had to tell my family about where I got the bruises, black eyes, and busted lips was ridiculous. The crazy thing is, I continued to stay with him. In some way, I felt like I deserved it. My whole life, I had been treated like I was nothing. Why should I move on? I felt like this guy was right. Maybe I was worthless and didn't deserve to live. In 2013, I checked into a hotel and at his prodding, took an overdose of medication. I just wanted to end all the pain I was feeling. I ended up leaving the hotel and tried to drive home but had to call 911 because I was so afraid.

I ended up staying in a behavioral health clinic for five days. After that, things went further south. I started partying, doing any kind of drug I could get my hands on and received attention from guys in wrong and shameful ways. I stopped going to church. I stopped reading God's Word. Praying wasn't habitual anymore and the only thing I could think of was my next fix. I had officially hit the rockiest parts of rock bottom. Driving my friends around for 10 hours a day to deliver drugs and to pick up drugs was my new job. I barely slept and I barely ate. From 2013 to almost 2015, I tried to fill the void in my heart by replacing my love for God with drugs.

Looking back, it's by the grace of God I was able to walk away from it all. I woke up one morning, hungover and feeling like absolute garbage. I told everyone that they needed to leave my apartment. I never hung out with those people again. I went back to my church, started seeking God, and had my foot back in the door to getting back to fixing my relationship with God.

Unfortunately, I still felt a void in my soul that I didn't let God fill. So I tried to fill it myself by finding a guy who liked me. At least I thought he did. He appeared to be what I was looking for, he came to church with me...but fast-forward, I became pregnant by him and everything changed when I told him.

I have been a single mom for exactly four years now, and I love every moment. Even through difficult "mom" times, I wouldn't trade this for anything. My child is so loved and wanted. The bottom line is, even though I have searched for love in all the wrong ways, Jesus never fails me. Even though I've been insecure my whole life, I am reminded that I am "more precious than jewels." And even though I have disappointed my family, myself, and even God, my heart will always be mended by His steadfast love. But God.

This. This is my story of redemption. I am a child of God.

DECREES

1. I decree God is restoring lost purpose and I am reclaiming His purpose, His thesis, for my life and the lives of my prodigals.

2. I call back my prodigal and decree their destiny will be fulfilled. Their purpose will not be cut off.

3. I decree my future and the future of my prodigal is good.

4. I decree God's Word is an anchor for my soul. I shall not be moved.

5. I decree God's Word is unshakable and will not return void. It will accomplish its purpose.

6. I decree my prodigal was created for God, His hand is on your life, we call forth the destiny and purpose God ordained for you.

7. I decree the steadfast love of the Lord never ceases. His mercies are new every morning.

8. I decree that even when I can't see it or feel it, God is working behind the scenes to bring my loved one home.

9. I decree God's amazing love and presence is overwhelming my prodigal and there is no escaping Him and His plan for your life.

10. I decree awakening in my prodigal, eyes to be opened, and heart to be receptive.

Note

1. All references to *Strong's* regarding Greek/Hebrew word translations are taken from *Strong's Exhaustive Concordance of the Bible* by James Strong; https://www .biblehub.com/strongs.htm; accessed September 8, 2023.

2

ANGELS OF
EVANGELISM

God's purposes are coming together in supernaturally accelerated ways. Promises, dreams, visions, and prophecies are surging into this moment. God invites us to participate in His purposes through prayer, faith decrees, worship, and embracing who we really are—sons and daughters who use their authority to reign with Christ in this life, as Paul says in Romans 5:17.

Recently, Holy Spirit said to me:

> *"Now begins the merger of Christ's spiritual Kingdom in the earth realm with the Kingdom of Heaven in the spirit realm in ways and levels never seen before. The merger will accelerate a new-era Pentecost. Power and Kingdom authority will be seen on the earth as never seen before. I'm merging the Kingdom of Heaven with you and pouring out My Spirit in far greater measure. I am giving you assistance I've given no other generation. I have made you to work with My angels at levels no other generation has done."*

This would include angelic assistance in reaching our prodigals.

I believe Holy Spirit is now pouring out power from Heaven at a level which has never occurred before. Just as the prophet Joel said was going to happen in Joel 2:28, and which Peter repeated in Acts 2:17. Another great awakening and reformation is now beginning. Another great outpouring, greater than all of them put together, is in process—and this time it will be assisted by more of the angel armies, more so than in any other outpouring.

Acts 2:17-18 (NKJV) says:

And it shall come to pass in the last days, says God, that I will pour out of My Spirit on all flesh; your sons and your daughters shall prophesy, your young men shall see visions, your old men shall dream dreams. And on My menservants and on My maidservants I will pour out My Spirit in those days; and they shall prophesy.

What a promise to the heirs. We must declare boldly, fueling angels with faith-filled decrees. This is a hope-filled word that is activating right now on this planet for the heirs and for their families. God has promised an outpouring on all flesh. That includes our sons and daughters, our grandchildren, our great-grandchildren, and our prodigals.

Clearly, hell has made an all-out effort to stop this great out-pouring. It has made attempts to teach children godless principles through media, big tech, education, arts, and entertainment. It has tried to propagandize them with demon ideas and doctrines of devils—from abortion acceptance to a homosexual lifestyle. To program them to think the same, act the same and live lives based on their foolish lies and deceptions.

While I know and am thankful for many great, dedicated edu-cators, there are others who are teaching demon doctrine, such as accepting body mutilation, gender confusion, and "woke" ideologies. Many of our nation's colleges and universities are now cesspools filled with ideas taught by perverts who seek to destroy the coming generation's creative potential and make them mindless lemmings who will follow their lies without ques-tion. "Don't think for yourself. We'll think for you. Just do what we say and think how we think."

Some of our schools have even attempted to remove parental influence over their children. Why? So they can teach perversion, witchcraft, the antichrist agenda, and identity politics. Many of their textbooks are filled with this perversion.

Our children have been taught socialism, communism, Marxism, Nazism, racism, and other crazy "isms." Yes it's lunacy, but there are some lunatics with the children all day long. If parents protest against the radical indoctrination, they are labeled by the union as domestic terrorists. Sadly, our own Department of Justice has also declared these parents to be domestic terrorists.

The overall level of education in the United States of America of industrialized nations is down to 27th on the list.[1] We haven't been teaching our students the skills they need. They've been indoctrinated. There has been an attempt to destroy the personalities of our children in a maze of demonic twisted deception that will lead them to be easily manipulated subjects of the deep state and of tyrannical government.

But please hear the word and promise of the Lord. Hear the One who never lies:

> *"There will rise a glorious Ekklesia that will do what He says, how He says to do it. There will rise a glorious Ekklesia who will lead a stand for change. There will rise a remnant warrior army of saints on earth who will change things; and angel armies will assist them, led by Lord Sabaoth."*

EVANGELISM ANGELS AND THE HARVEST

...the harvest is the end of the age, and the reapers are the angels.

(Matthew 13:39 NKJV)

Jesus said a sign of the end times and His coming would be angels becoming reapers. There are at least two angels assigned to every person at birth (Matthew 18:10). Their assignment is to pull out the destiny God has planned for them. Your angels are briefed on your destiny and they work to bring it out of you. You may rebel against that destiny, but the angels are not going to stop trying until you die (see Chapter 5 in *Angel Armies*).

The division of evangelism angels help to draw destiny out of people and, of most importance, they draw you to Christ. You must be born again. There are three phases in this division.

Phase 1: The Prodigals

Millions of prodigals are about to come home. Many of them were raised in church and they know their Bible. We need to get them home and plugged in. I am convinced some of the greatest apostles, pastors, and ministers in this new era are prodigals who are returning to the church. I list this category first because we have to have them and because there has been a billion-soul harvest prophesied. I was in Chicago a few years ago and prophesied that the greatest exodus in history would not be the exodus of the million souls Moses led out of Egyptian bondage. Rather, it would be an exodus of a billion souls leaving worldly bondage and returning to their roots in this new era.

Phase 2: New Converts

Brand-new, born-again ones are coming in. It's harvest time and evangelism angels are assisting in the harvest of new souls coming into the Kingdom of God.

Phase 3: Evangelists

The fivefold ministry office of an evangelist will be restored and connected to apostolic hubs. This office has to function and we need present-day "Billy Grahams" to come forth. The potential is unlimited and what we are about to see take place in the body of Christ is incredible.

I believe our sons and daughters are going to prophesy. Our sons and daughters are going to dream the dream of their God. Holy Spirit is going to pour out His power from Heaven to change them, heal their minds, and cleanse their drug-fogged thinking to realign and reset their hearts and reactivate their purpose. Holy Spirit is going to awaken them—spirit, soul, and body—and purge demon confusion from them with the truth that sets them free.

Our prodigals are not too far gone. The arm of the Lord is not short. He can reach them. They are not a hopeless cause. They are not unredeemable. They have not fallen too far. They are not too confused to come to their senses. That's a demon lie. Power is coming to liberate them. The power of the living God is coming to explode the demon doctrines and confusion and set them free.

Their destinies are not lost. What God planned for each one of them before they were ever born will not be stolen from them. Believe and decree what God says. Fight for what God says and make a stand for the children, for the coming generation. They are part of the billion soul harvest. A Jesus Movement is now in process that is far greater than the Jesus Movement in the 1960s, '70s, and early '80s. What a great movement that was, but that will pale in comparison to what God has planned for now.

You can mark it down. There are some demonized people who have brought great harm to children who, unless there is repentance, will face God putting millstones around their necks. An Ekklesia must rise and unashamedly say what God says. We must say it. We must vote for biblical values. We must stand for it. We must fight. We must boldly rise and make a public stand against the sexual exploitation of children, the teaching of critical race theory (CRT), gender confusion, woke agendas, and other craziness.

We must make our stand. Our kids will not be pronoun puppets for the world's insanity. They will not be the lab kids for evil to experiment on with its sick agenda. They are not gender confused. They are our sons and daughters. We are their mothers and their fathers, not DNA donors. Where the world has made attempts, we must stand and take authority in the Name of Jesus. We must decree and declare that our children are destined to be who God says they are.

We trust what Jesus said in Matthew 18:6 (AMPC):

> *But whoever causes one of these little ones who believe in and acknowledge and cleave to Me to stumble and sin [that is, who entices him or hinders him in right conduct or thought], it would be better (more expedient and profitable or advantageous) for him to have a great millstone fastened around his neck and to be sunk in the depth of the sea.*

I didn't say that, the King of kings said it. Those who are purposefully leading children from Christ's teaching will find that God never lies. Evil will lose its voice and there are going to be consequences—and the angels are going to help us get that done.

An outpouring of the Holy Spirit has begun. It's in process and growing in greater and greater measure right in front of our eyes. It's an outpouring that is empowering the true church to stand and change things. It's coming to set our sons, daughters, and grandkids free. Multiplied millions of them around the world are going to become passionate, Spirit-filled believers running with their God-given destinies. Our prodigals are coming home.

What a magnificent promise is set before the heirs who believe what God says and His promise. Intensify your prayers for the coming generation. An awesome promise, assisted by mighty angels, is coming to help set a targeted generation free, who will dream God's dream and prophesy His Word. That's what God says.

PROPHETIC WORD

"I am rewriting the story of the downcast, the bruised, the forsaken, the wounded, and the captives. Their witness of Me shall be My declaration throughout the ages. I am the Lord mighty to save."

PRAYER

Lord, I pray for an outpouring of Your Spirit on our sons, daughters, grandchildren, and great-grandchildren. I pray that a Jesus Movement greater than any other will begin to sweep this land and around the world. I bind lying spirits. I bind evil communication. The angels of God are here to assist us in taking back a mighty part of our harvest. Our children will sing Your songs. Our children will dream Your dreams. Our children will minister under the anointing of Your Holy Spirit. They will be mighty members of Your Kingdom. Hell will not stop it.

I pray, God, that Your angels would assist this word around this planet now. Let the prophets, apostles, and intercessors hear. Let the decree go forth. It is time.

Let there be an outpouring of Your Holy Spirit that will bring light into the darkness the enemy has tried to wrap around their minds and set them free. Let truth penetrate darkness. Let light shine upon the way to go. Let the calling voice of the Father resonate deep inside their being, through the fog of drugs or alcohol, through the fog of demon teachings. Light their souls with the purpose that You have in mind for them.

I thank You for all of Your promises and we decree we will embrace these promises. We will fight for them. Angels will hear our voices declaring freedom to the coming generation, declaring with authority, "You cannot have them! No weapon formed against them is going to prosper. The watchmen will rise and you will be defeated."

Let it accelerate according to Your plans and we will steward it as best we can under the Holy Spirit. In Jesus's name. Amen.

DECREES

1. We decree angels are being released to assist in bringing all generations home.

2. We decree harvest is now and prodigals are returning to the Father.

3. We declare angels are working with us to see destiny accomplished in and through our children. We say destiny is *not* lost and will *not* be stolen from them.

4. We decree a Jesus Movement has begun and an outpouring released over our sons, daughters, and our grandchildren.

5. We decree our children will sing Your songs and dream Your dreams. They will prophesy.

6. We declare we will make our stand and reclaim our land and angel armies will assist.

7. We decree great leaders from the coming generation are rising to take their place in the King's Ekklesia.

8. We decree supernatural encounters with King Jesus are accelerating.

9. We decree prodigals are coming to their senses, realizing they have been lied to by the enemy, and are returning home.

10. **We decree Jeremiah 24:7 (NIV):** *"I will give them a heart to know me, that I am the Lord. They will be my people, and I will be their God, for they will return to me with all their heart."*

Note

1. Aria Bendix, "The US was once a leader for healthcare and education—now it ranks 27th in the world," *Business Insider*, September 27, 2018; https://www.businessinsider.com/ us-ranks-27th-for-healthcare-and-education-2018-9; accessed September 7, 2023.

HOPE SINGS

3

HOPE SINGS

A TESTIMONY (ANONYMOUS)

I never thought I would find myself writing something like this.

My husband and I raised our children in church. We were there for every service. They attended Sunday school, Bible clubs, VBS, youth meetings, camps, and any other activity the church offered. We started them out in Christian preschool and elementary school. At home, I planned fun activities that often included Christian or moral lessons. At a very young age, both children accepted Jesus as their Savior. We were thrilled. Life was good. We had succeeded as Christian parents. Our kids were saved; they were going to Heaven. We did it!

Until...my world fell apart. One of my children (married now, with children of her own) dropped a bombshell into our lives. She no longer considered herself a Christian. At this writing, she and her husband are no longer serving the Lord or raising their kids in the church. Even typing this, I am feeling all the emotions this revelation caused when she first told me this: sadness, disappointment, anger, fear, embarrassment. I find myself cycling in and out of these emotions on a regular basis. I also cycle in and out of hope that they'll come to their senses and return to the God of their childhood (both she and her husband were raised in church).

I've had the sleepless nights, the tear-stained pillow, the muffled sobbing as I've prayed and pleaded with God to somehow miraculously turn this around. I've been angry at God, as if it's His fault. After all, I did everything right, didn't I? I raised them right! How did this happen?!

Now I'm watching from afar as they live a life clearly not centered on God or the church. We're not estranged; we're still a close family. But it's awkward now. They don't want to hear about God. I'm finding myself censoring my comments, suppressing my true feelings, withholding comments such as, "I'll be praying for you," or "God's got this."

I would have to say that fear is one of the biggest emotions I'm experiencing. Fear that they'll never turn back to God. Fear that my grandchildren will never be saved. Fear that I'll die before it ever happens. I'm always wondering if I should leave a note for after my death, pleading with them to accept Jesus so we'll meet again in Heaven. Thoughts like these can cause one to go down a dangerous path, because I KNOW that I shouldn't be fearful. I remind myself that God pursued me when I was a teenager and He's still in the pursuing business.

I know the Scriptures. I know that God died for my daughter. I know I did my due diligence in raising her. I know God has a plan and a purpose for her and her family. I know I'm not the Savior; He is. I know God hasn't given me a spirit of fear; I know that's from the enemy. But when in a desperate situation, when deep in the battle, when you find yourself weary and growing faint, losing hope, you need help!

That's where this book comes in. I don't need to be sobbing into my pillow and losing hope. I need to stand up and face the enemy. I need the words to decree that my daughter WILL return to the Lord! That the devil is a LIAR! That no weapon formed against my daughter and her family will prosper! I remind myself of these words in Ephesians 3:20 (MSG): *"God can do anything, you know—far more than you could ever imagine or guess or request in your wildest dreams! He does it not by pushing us around but by working within us, his Spirit deeply and gently within us."* I remind myself that this is exactly how I came to know the Lord as a teenager, while attending a revival in a small storefront church. Holy Spirit began gently speaking into my heart during one of the services and I couldn't run to the altar fast enough to give my heart to Jesus. I have to believe that He is working in my daughter and her family's hearts, as well. It is not up to me to save them, but it IS up to me to pray and decree!

Our words matter. The Bible is full of good promises for us and for our prodigals. I'm ready to face the enemy and take back what has been stolen from me, and what he has stolen from my daughter and her family. The devil CANNOT and WILL NOT have my family. Even though my daughter is grown and no longer living in our household, I have always quoted and dwelled upon this verse:

As for me and my family, we'll worship God.

(Joshua 24:15 MSG)

I also think about what the apostle Paul wrote to Timothy concerning Timothy's faith:

*That precious memory triggers another: your honest faith—and what a rich faith it is, handed down from your **grandmother** Lois to your **mother** Eunice, and now to you!*

(2 Timothy 1:5 MSG)

I remind myself that my husband and I dedicated our children to the Lord, we raised them in the fear and knowledge of Him, and we (all of us!) WILL worship the Lord. We have passed down our faith and we refuse to let the enemy steal our children and grandchildren. They belong to God!

BIBLICAL HOPE

Now let's consider biblical hope:

I am convinced that some of my most powerful prayers weren't spoken in words, but tears. **—Anonymous**

During one of David's darkest and most fearful times, he prayed these words, "*You keep track of all my sorrows. You have collected all my tears in your bottle. You have recorded each one in your book*" (Psalm 56:8 NLT).

If you are the parent, relative, or friend of a prodigal, you have likely shed enough tears to fill a bottle and then some. Your heart is grieved that someone you love more than life itself has turned their back on God and possibly you as well. You may be tormenting yourself with thoughts of things you could have done differently and thinking of all the "what ifs." You likely have felt heavy sadness, anger, embarrassment, or shame. There are not enough words to describe the fear, disappointment, and hopelessness you feel at times.

When you look at things in the natural, it can be easy to become discouraged and start thinking that what you are doing is in vain. You can often become weary in the waiting and doubt begins to creep in, but just one spark of hope is all it takes to start believing and expecting again.

Scripture consistently tells us to set our hope on God and on Christ. First Peter 1:3 (NIV) says that *Jesus is our Living Hope*. Romans 5:5 says that *hope does not disappoint us,* and in Romans 8, Paul speaks of waiting with eager expectation. Hebrews 6:18-19 mentions *taking refuge by seizing the sure anchor of hope that is set before us*. We have a hope and the hope we have in Jesus is an anchor to our soul. That means hope doesn't float on the surface of your situation, but it gets down to the bottom and holds on tight.

In Romans 8 we read about the nature of hope:

> *For we know that the whole creation groans and labors with birth pangs together until now. Not only that, but we also who have the firstfruits of the Spirit, even we ourselves groan within ourselves, eagerly waiting for the adoption, the redemption of our body. For we were saved in this hope, but hope that is seen is not hope; for why does one still hope for what he sees? But if we hope for what we do not see, we eagerly wait for it with perseverance.*
> **(Romans 8:22-25 NKJV)**

The word *hope* in this text is *elpis* (Strong's 1680). It means a desire for some future good with the expectation of obtaining it. *Hope is confident expectancy. Hope* in Scripture is not the world's definition. The world defines hope as wishing something would happen. The world's definition says, "I hope this will happen, but I don't really know if it will." Biblical hope is different. Biblical hope is the looking forward to something with absolute confidence, expecting fulfillment. When we're tempted to be downcast by our circumstances, we can gain Heaven's perspective by looking up to God and being filled with the kind of hope that can only come from Him.

EAGERLY WAITING WITH CONFIDENCE

Romans 8:25 says if we hope for what we do not see, we eagerly wait for it with perseverance. I know it's basic, but we're not hoping for what we already see. We hope for what we do not see. "We hope" is the word *elpizo*, which means to look forward with confidence to that which is good and beneficial (Strong's 1679). The present tense of this word pictures this attitude as the believer's lifestyle—one of hope. Hope is defined as the absolute assurance that God will do good to us and for us in the future.

W.E. Vine writes, "It is not merely a trust in God, but it's a hope that rests upon Him."

We have a certain hope that rests in God. Even when we don't yet see what we're hoping for, we have a confidence that should prompt a specific attitude and behavior within us. An attitude that says, "I know in whom I believe and my hope rests in Him." No matter what I see in the life of my prodigal, my hope is in God.

66

Eagerly waiting means waiting in great anticipation and wait-ing with patience, to expect fully. Oftentimes, we say, "I'm just going to wait it out," or "I'm going to wait this out with patience." A person with this kind of hope can persevere or bear up under whatever their circumstance is because they have a fixed confi-dence that knows what is coming.

It's this kind of biblical hope that allows us to declare with confidence Philippians 1:6 (MSG): *"...There has never been the slightest doubt in my mind that the God who started this great work in you, would keep at it and bring it to a flourishing finish."*

Hope is the proper response to the promises of God. When walking under the overwhelming weight of dark moments, yet still allowing hope in. Like light that slips through the crack of a door into a darkened room, let hope seep into your heart and soul.

Zephaniah 3:17 (NKJV) says, *"The Lord your God in your midst, the Mighty One, will save; He will rejoice over you with glad-ness, He will quiet you with His love, He will rejoice over you with singing."*

The Lord our God sings over us; and because Jesus is our Living Hope, we know that hope also sings over us and it over-whelms the darkness. As a believer, to not hope, to not trust or not believe simply isn't an option.

You have an established history with the King. He is your Savior and Redeemer, so you have firsthand knowledge of His goodness and saving grace. Believe He will save your prodigal.

Psalm 27:13-14 (KJV) says, *"I had fainted, unless I had believed to see the goodness of the Lord in the land of the living. Wait on the Lord: be of good courage, and he shall strengthen thine heart: wait, I say, on the Lord."* These verses were written by David, a man who demonstrated great faith in our God.

David had an assurance that no matter what difficulties and dangers stalked his path, God would come to rescue him, and he simply had to wait confidently for the Lord to act. *Be strong, he wrote, and let your heart take courage; and, wait for the Lord.*

David, who killed the great giant Goliath and who was honored as the one who slew tens of thousands, admitted that without trust in his God, his heart would faint, and he would despair. Hope in his God was to David a soothing ointment that eased his flagging spirit. It became a refreshing, heavenly hope that ministered to his mind, calmed his emotions, and revitalized his fainting heart.

David determined in his heart that even if a host encamped against him, his heart would not fear. If war broke out against him, and his enemies tried to devour him, his confidence in God would stand fast.

THE EYE OF FAITH

The eye of faith is to see beyond the visible and to discern the invisible. It is to maintain an unswerving assurance that the promises of God are all "Yes" and "Amen" in Christ Jesus. It is to trust the Lord our God with all our heart for what we have hoped for and the evidence of the reality of what can only be seen with the eye of faith.

Believing in the waiting can be very difficult. It's often in the middle of circumstances when the accuser begins to attack your mind and attempt to wear you down with hopelessness. You begin to think that prayers for your unsaved or lost loved one are in vain.

Think of the story of the children of Israel walking in the wilderness for 40 years. One thing was between them and their land of promise—the Jordan River. The Lord stopped the flow of the river, so the Israelites could cross. When they finally entered the Promised Land, Joshua and his twelve men built a memorial of stones. This would be a reminder of what God did for them.

It is interesting to note what happens next. Joshua 4:9 (NLT) says, *"Joshua also set up another pile of twelve stones in the middle of the Jordan, at the place where the priests who carried the Ark of the Covenant were standing. And they are there to this day."*

There are two sets of stones, two memorials. One set in the Promised Land and one *right in the middle* of the Jordan. What happens to us in the middle shapes us. You may be in the middle of praying, waiting, and believing for your prodigal. It is important to look back and see memorials of God's faithfulness in your life in order to build your faith.

There are many things in my life that I have had to believe, pray, and contend for. I went through an intense time of needing to see God's healing power in my family's life. For me personally, I could have built memorials of loss, defeat, hopelessness, and bitterness. While I was faithfully contending for the healing of my daughter, I could have easily said things such as, "Well, now we have to go through something else; here comes another diagnosis; now we're suffering another loss; here comes troubled waters again."

THE MIDDLE

The middle can feel really long, but things are happening that we tend to forget. We need to learn to build a memorial not just in the end, but also in the middle. The middle is the peak of your vulnerability where you're tempted to quit. It's when the overwhelming feelings of sadness, anger and shame can threaten to overwhelm—but God trains us in the middle. The middle of what you'd never choose, can propel you into a Promised Land you'd never know.

I never would have chosen to go through infertility and lose baby after baby. But then I never would have received the redemptive plan of adoption, which now I wouldn't trade for all the world. God was working a beautiful plan and turning things for good, even when I couldn't see it. He is also working in the heart of your prodigal. Even when you can't see it, trust that He is working.

There are also some memorial stones that are just between you and Jesus. There are some moments that only Jesus knows about. Times when He whispered to your heart things you needed to hear. Times when He infused you with strength to get through the moment. Times when He, the Living Hope, sang over you.

The Lord told Joshua to set up twelve stones after crossing the Jordan. Then Joshua ran back to the riverbed, before the waters came back together and placed his own twelve stones right on that dry ground. He placed the stones and said to God, *"I will never ever forget what You did in the middle."*

In 1 Samuel 17, Goliath was mocking the Israelites, then David came and said that the giant could be defeated. Everyone thought David was out of his mind, but David remembered his memorials. He remembered the time he fought a lion and bear and even though no one else knew about it, he had an established history with God (see 1 Samuel 17:34-37).

You may be one who also has memorials no one knows but God. Perhaps you can say, "I have fought a lion and a bear in the secret places where no one knows. When the enemy came to attack or when he came for my children, but God is mighty to save."

THE SECRET PLACE

You become a warrior in the secret place. Fighting when no one was watching but God. Don't forget what God did for you in the middle. In the middle, He shapes you and teaches you. Mark 6:47-51 assures us that Jesus is good at entering right into the middle of an angry wave. In the middle of that storm, Jesus walked right in and said, "Don't be afraid, I am here."

Be assured that you won't always be in the middle. Whatever you are going through will come to an end. Everyone around you may forget what you went through, but you'll remember because you laid the stones. You built the memorial and you made the memories, just you and Jesus standing in the middle.

A people after God's heart keep a constant spirit of hope. He is the God who makes ways when there seems to be no way, and He makes the impossible, possible.

A few years ago when our family was walking through a difficult situation, Holy Spirit said to me: *Do not give false power to present circumstances.* As I pondered what that meant, I realized He was telling me the power I was handing over about this circumstance was in the wrong hands. So my next thought was obviously the power for whatever I am facing is in God. It's in His hands.

I wrote out this following statement and it became a daily prayer: *"I will not give false power, which is control, authority, or influence, to present circumstances. I will instead decree the power or the capacity, aptitude, authority, mighty and wonderful works of God."*

Our present circumstances don't define our future, which is one reason why you can't give power over to current situations.

The situation doesn't hold the power, God does, when we give it to Him. Renew your mind to see the good and be filled with hope. Remind yourself of who God is and that He alone holds the power.

> *And what is the exceeding greatness of His power toward us who believe, according to the working of His mighty power.*
> **(Ephesians 1:19 NKJV)**

God holds the whole ocean in His hands, and He created the land on which we stand and walk. This same power is available to us today.

God is the power who created the heavens and the earth. When He said, *"Let there be light!"* the light came to the earth, and He created day and night (Genesis 1),

We see further examples of God's power in Exodus 14:21 when He parted the Red Sea; in Joshua 6:20 when He made the walls of Jericho fall without a single blow; and Joshua 10:13 tells us that *even the sun and the moon have to stand still at His command.* God is infinitely great.

Have you not known? Have you not heard? The everlasting God, the Lord, the Creator of the ends of the earth, neither faints nor is weary. His understanding is unsearchable. He gives power to the weak, and to those who have no might He increases strength.
(Isaiah 40:28-29 NKJV)

The Bible says that the faith of any believer should not be founded in religious reasoning, but on the power of God:

My message and my preaching were not with persuasive words of human wisdom, but in demonstration of the Spirit and of power, that your faith should not be in the wisdom of men, but in the power of God.
(1 Corinthians 2:4-5 NKJV)

We can discuss and reason all our life, but when the power of God touches and transforms us, then we know with every part of our being that God is real, that He loves us, and that He wants to heal and save us. We must lay hold of faith in God's power in our personal lives.

This power is strong enough to set us free from sin and bring us into a life of abiding in the will of God. This powerful truth is what gives us a future and hope.

Jesus, the Living Hope, is singing over you, your family, your loved ones, and your prodigals. It's a song of love, mercy, hope, redemption, and saving grace.

Hope Is Rising

Song by Rachel Shafer

Hope sings its song to me

And I can't help but believe

It's singing a melody

Washing right over me

Hope is singing

Hope is rising

Out of the dark, from the depths of my soul

Hope rises up saying, "Don't you let go

The waves and the wind still know My voice

It's time to praise, it's time to rejoice."

DECREES

1. I know in whom I believe, and I stand with confident expectation that God is working all for good in the life of my prodigal.

2. I decree that Jesus is my Living Hope, therefore I will never give up, for hope does not disappoint.

3. I decree that because of my history with Jesus, I know He is mighty to save. My prodigal will be saved in Jesus's Name.

4. I decree God will redeem and restore. He loves my prodigal even more than I do.

5. I will not give false power—control, authority, or influence—to present circumstances. I will instead decree the power or the capacity, aptitude, authority, mighty, and wonderful works of God.

6. I decree my prodigal will be surrounded by godly influences and by those who exemplify and promote Your ways, truths, and values.

7. I decree anything that is dangerous or not in Your will to be removed from the lives of prodigals. I decree You will bring them out of darkness and break any chains that have them bound.

8. I shake off all doubt, depression, and heart sickness that would cause me to be hope-deferred. I stand strong on the faithfulness of God.

9. I lift high the power of the cross over my prodigal's life and stake it in the ground of their mind, will, and emotions. I exalt the Name of Jesus and apply His blood to the places in their hearts and minds that harbor false beliefs.

10. I decree God will make the valley of trouble into a door of hope (Hosea 2:14-15). I trust You, knowing You have already made a way. My prodigal is coming home.

EXHORTATION OF HOPE

Be strengthened in the Name of the Lord, through His power and His might. We declare His faithfulness over you. Stand strong, and never give up. Let hope rise up. We bind all fear the enemy would try to harass you with and we speak peace over you, and we speak renewed energy and new fortitude to press on. Never give up. Know that God loves your prodigal even more than you do, and He is dancing over them with His love. He is always working behind the scenes; keep speaking His Word and plant the heavens, giving the angels something to work with. Give the Lord thanks every day for what He is doing, no matter what you see or feel.

4

I WILL SAVE YOUR CHILDREN

Something very significant, which has been prayed about for decades, is beginning to accelerate throughout the earth. The Godhead is up to something; I feel the synergy of it, the wind upon it. I sense the anointing of the Holy Spirit, and I can see prophetic words coming together. Somehow, deep in my innermost being, I perceive it. As we used to say, "I know it in my knower!"

I want to share prophetic insight that I feel is important for our present times. Holy Spirit has prophesied to us, for many years now, that multiple movements will begin to rise in the earth realm. I have seen, in vision form, a wave of revival, like a tsunami type of wave, that just kept coming and coming and building and building.

These movements will merge together in a mighty move of God, the likes of which have never been seen before. It will be a Holy Spirit outpouring that is even greater than the one that occurred in Acts 2. We know that only 120 people had gathered in the upper room, waiting for that first outpouring of Holy Spirit. The upcoming outpouring, however, will affect millions of people. Not only will the outpouring itself be greater, but it's going to touch *all* flesh, as the prophet Joel prophesied in Joel 2:28, and which the apostle Peter repeated on the day of Pentecost in Acts 2:16-21. God said it would come upon all flesh, all races, all people groups, all ages, male and female.

> *...I will pour out my Spirit upon all people. Your sons and daughters will prophesy. Your old men will dream dreams, and your young men will see visions. In those days I will pour out my Spirit even on servants—men and women alike. And I will cause wonders in the heavens and on the earth....*
>
> **(Joel 2:28-30 NLT)**

The Hebrew word for *prophesy* is *naba* (Strong's 5012) and it means to speak God's message under Holy Spirit's influence. Our sons and daughters are going to speak God's message under Holy Spirit influence. *Naba* also means to represent God's plan, His will, or His ways in words or songs.

Singing will be a big part of this present-day revival, just as it was in the 1960s and '70s with the Jesus Movement that I came up through. Singing groups were popping up everywhere back then. My wife, Carol, and I were even in a singing group called Paraclete for a couple of years. We were good!

What were these singing groups doing? They were singing the Bible, proclaiming God's Word. These songs became the contemporary music that we often hear today. Up until that point, hymns were prominent, but spontaneous worship began to occur and people would start singing songs from their hearts. They would sing verses they had read in the Bible. This outpouring will be no different. The Word of God is going to be emphasized, it's going to be sung, and spontaneous worship and prayer will be an integral part of it.

In Joel 2:23, Joel prophesied that an era of outpourings would occur when the former and the latter rains would come simultaneously, or at the same time. This is significant. Rain, in the Scriptures, often represents revival, or outpourings, of the Holy Spirit. The springtime rains were the planting rains that watered the seeds that had been sown. The harvest rains, which were seven times greater than the springtime rains, ripened the harvest for reaping. Joel prophesied that both types of rains were going to come and happen at the same time:

> *Be glad then, ye children of Zion, and rejoice in the Lord your God: for he hath given you the former rain*

moderately, and he will cause to come down for you the rain, the former rain, and the latter rain in the first month.

(Joel 2:23 KJV)

The prophet Amos prophesied it this way in Amos 9:13-15 (NKJV), *"'Behold the day has come,' says the Lord, 'when the plowman will overtake the reaper, and the treader of grapes him who sows seeds.'"* The Message Bible declares, *"God's Decree. Things are going to happen so fast your head will swim, one thing fast on the heels of the other. You won't be able to keep up. Everything will be happening at once—and everywhere you look, blessings! Blessings like wine pouring off the mountains and hills."*

The type of revival that we are currently seeing take place is like that. You can't keep up with it. "It's here!" "No, it's there!" "Well, it's starting in that place!" It's accelerating and spreading quickly.

I believe that Amos 9:13-15 is referencing the first worldwide Kingdom revival that has ever been seen. It's not going to be like the revivals in the past. I praise God for the Brownsville and Toronto revivals. I attended both and enjoyed them. But it is not God's plan in this era for us to have to travel thousands of miles to be in revival.

The revivals we have seen taking place in some of our colleges—Asbury, Lee University, Cedarville, and many others—will spread to hundreds of places. There will be way too many for hell to stop! And not just in Christian colleges, but also secular ones, high schools, churches, youth groups, Ekklesias in all 50 states and nations of the world. Hell is not going to be able to contain it. That's what God said.

The prophet Isaiah gives us a great promise that I believe we need to embrace right now in our times:

> *Who can snatch the plunder of war from the hands of a warrior? Who can demand that a tyrant let his captives go? But the Lord says, "The captives of warriors will be released, and the plunder of tyrants will be retrieved. For I will fight those who fight you, and **I will save your children.**"*

> **(Isaiah 49:24-25 NLT)**

Several other words for *retrieved* are *gotten back, recovered, restored.* Joel prophesied in Joel 2:25 (KJV) that the years that the locust, cankerworm, caterpillar, and palmerworm have eaten, God was going to restore. These pests were grub worms that would eat the harvest. God was literally saying that He was going to restore His people's lost harvests. How many harvests (prodigals) have we lost? Millions and millions, and that's why we prophesy a billion souls are coming in. They're going to be recovered. God is going to fight those who fight us, and He is going to save our children.

There are evil cultural warriors promoting iniquity and perversion in our society. Tyrants have sought to capture our children with confusing lies and distorted ideology. There are those who think they are giants, too big for us to stop them from indoctrinating our children with demon ideas, who are about to discover that God is at war with them.

They will soon realize they are contending with Almighty God and they cannot beat Him. Our God is saying to us, "*I will contend with those who contend with My people. I will fight those who fight you. I'm on your side and I will defend your cause. I will take the plunder of war away from them and I will deliver those who are held captive. I will save your children; I will rescue them."*

The Hebrew word for *contend* is *ruwb* (Strong's 7378) and it means to grapple, to defend, to grab someone by the hair of the head. It means to fight with words, to fight physically, legal combat through laws, and it is sometimes used as the word in the Old Testament for ambush. It sounds to me like God means business!

Perhaps that is why Jesus says in Matthew 18:6 (The Passion Translation), *"If anyone abuses one of these little ones who believes in me, it would be better for him to have a heavy boulder tied around his neck and be hurled into the deepest sea than to face the punishment he's deserved."*

The Hebrew word for *save* is *yasha* (Strong's 3467) and it means to free, to avenge, to rescue, to save physically and soul-ishly. It was very interesting to me to study this word. The Hebrew scholars say *yasha* was specifically pointed toward the healing of emotions, or it referenced healing for someone's emotional state.

The coming generation has been traumatized these past few years. Fears have oppressed them. Covid and ridiculous lock-downs have affected so many of our children to the point that some of them are suffering with depression and are on drugs for that. Depression is plaguing hundreds of thousands of American children.

But God says, *"I'm going to pour out My Spirit and change things. I'm going to avenge them and I'm going to heal their emotions. I'm going to heal their souls. I'm going to fight those who teach them demon doctrine. I'm going to wrestle with those who lie to them, exploiting their innocence. I'm going to contend and I'm going to save them."*

Isaiah 49:25 (AMPC) says, *"...I will contend with him who contends with you, and I will give safety to your children and ease them."* We most certainly need to pray and decree this promise. I believe it is a promise that is in its moment. It's in the right time, which is now.

A week before our annual Prophetic Summit, I was in prayer for the coming generation. I have been, and continue to be, burdened for them. My heart breaks for our young people. Leading up to the Summit, I was praying for a change in the chaos our government and education system has caused our children to live in. I was praying to reverse the mess that nominal, woke religion has produced. I was praying to reverse the effects of fatherlessness and passive parenting that give children no moral compass.

Parents are no longer raising their kids in the fear and admonition of the Lord. Foolishly, they say things such as, "We'll just let our kids raise themselves. If they choose to serve God, fine, but we will let them grow up and make their own choice." We continually see this happen, especially in nominal (in name only) churches. I was praying to reverse the effects on innocent children from drag queens, homosexual perversion, gender confusion, doctrines of devils, and an anti-Christ agenda of Baal.

On February 8, 2023, two days before the Prophetic Summit, I was planning to head out to the lake at Caesar Creek State Park to pray. I often do this for our annual Summits and other major church events. I go get alone with God and just soak the upcoming events in a day of prayer.

Just before leaving for the lake on Wednesday morning, I began to feel I was missing something that I was supposed to prophesy at the Summit. I decided that I wouldn't go to the lake that day and would, instead, go the next day.

Carol said to me, "I thought you said you were ready for the Summit." And I replied, "Well, I thought I was, but now I feel there's something I don't have, so I'll just wait and go to the lake on Thursday to pray."

I went into my office and began to just quietly pray. I said, "Holy Spirit, what? Why did You stop me from going to the lake today?" I knew it was the Holy Spirit who had stayed me and I simply said, "I'm listening!"

I felt impressed to pray for the coming generation, for Gen Z, ages 15-25ish. As I prayed, I became very emotional, and after just a few moments, I heard God speak. They were words spoken so emphatically, yet with such love and compassion, that it caused my spirit to begin to shake inside of me, and I began to weep. Tears dripped down my cheeks, which is not normal for me (nothing wrong with it, it's just not typical for me). I only told two people, Carol and my brother, Dutch, the timing of this. I didn't want to interject myself into something. It was holy and precious, and I just wanted to pray into it, which I did, and continued to do, for many days afterward.

This prophetic download was given to me between 9:30 and 10:30 a.m. on Wednesday, February 8. The Asbury College revival began at 10 a.m. that same morning, in their chapel service. The word I was receiving and the Asbury outpouring began simultaneously, although I wouldn't hear about the revival breaking out until the next day. I feel that it could not be a coincidence and, more importantly, I feel it's confirming some things about this season, this era.

I knew Holy Spirit had stopped me that morning to give me a confirming word that awakening and revival would now spread throughout the earth. I gave that word at the Summit on Friday night, which was before any other places were in revival. At that point, it was only Asbury, and it was obvious that something God-planned was going on.

As I was praying in my office that Wednesday for the coming generation, I heard the following words. I wrote as quickly as I could, tears dripping down my face, not wanting to miss a single word. As young Christians sang and worshiped, praising God in Wilmore, Kentucky, I heard these words:

"Behold and understand the mysterious wisdom of the Godhead, destroying the works of the forever loser. See their vision for a new era unfolding. The earth realm has seen the entrance of King Jesus for two millennia at levels and in ways never seen before. Never anticipated by the loser and his fallen ones. The King's person and His ministry of redemption, salvation, and grace has been presented in the earth realm. His kingship declared above all powers. Holy Spirit, the Comforter, the Enabler, the Communicator, has been presented in the earth realm, filling the heirs with the presence and power of His person.

"Now see new expressions, new discoveries, new dimensions, greater revelation, and amplified levels of the Father's heart to those made in His image and likeness.

"Now see His fathering anointing released into the earth in glorious measures. Now see the greatness of Father's heart hovering and covering with His person, saying to a fatherless generation, I want you! I will be your Father. You will not be fatherless. You will not be confused. You will not be lost. I will be

your Father. You will know My love is set upon you. You will not be orphans. You will not be aimless. I will mentor you. My family will welcome you. My family will embrace you. My family will care for you. My family will raise you. You will not be lost. I will take you in. There are rooms in My house for you. There's a seat at My table for you.

"My fathering nature, My fathering heart, will heal you. My hovering presence will realign you. My presence will define you. I will transform you. My heart of love for you will bring clarity to your purpose. You will not be a "they" or a "whatever." You will be a son. You will be a daughter. You will be an heir, My heir. I will Father you. My family will train you. I will love you to your destiny. I will clear the confusion. I will clear the lies and I will bring from you true identity."

I heard Holy Spirit say:

"New levels and new expressions of Father's heart will now be presented and much of it is pointed at the coming generation. And His fathering anointing poured into the earth realm will break the yoke of abandonment. It's breaking. It's breaking. God is going to break it. The hearts of the fathers will turn to the children. Brokenness will be healed and millions will say, 'I am free! I have identity in Father's family. I am loved. Father's greatness surrounds me. I have purpose. I have meaning.'"

The era of transforming shifts will now begin. Father is going to reveal His greatness to the world, which includes prodigals and the coming generation. They're not going to be lost.

The synergizing triunity of the Godhead in divine oneness is going to answer the challenge of Baal, and earth's harvests are going to be reaped as a generation, a coming generation, will also be found going about the Father's business (see Luke 2:49 NKJV).

Our family, God's family, is growing exponentially. Hell can't confine it. It's going to happen so fast our heads are going to spin.

I remember at the Summit, praying a line that I think is applicable. It just came up out of my spirit and I knew it was the Holy Spirit speaking. I prayed it then, and I decree it today. I heard Him say, "Sin is no match for My mercy." Sin is no match for His mercy. It's no match for His lovingkindness. Sin is no match for His love. God is going to reach the prodigals. Champions are rising!

A TESTIMONY (ANONYMOUS)

I was raised in a minister's home. My parents pastored a church, as well as having a traveling ministry. I saw a lot of things in the church that bothered me and certainly had "people" experiences that caused me disappointment and anger. As a young child, it began to shape the way I looked at things and it wasn't all good. When I was just a little older, my parents went through a divorce which shattered our family. There were church fights I witnessed during this time and we were pretty much left penniless when all was said and done. I was bitter, confused, and deeply hurt. I wanted nothing to do with God or the church and poured all my time into sports as an escape. I lived my life with no relationship with Him, yet He never left me. Deep in my heart, I knew I wanted to turn back to Him, but my heart was hardened. It wasn't until much later, after I was married, that I began to allow my heart to be dealt with and softened, and I accepted an invitation to church. Under great conviction, I responded to the altar call, and God began to heal me of all the childhood trauma, from church hurt to our broken family, and He began a restoring process in me. I had returned to the God of my childhood.

I Have Returned

Words and Music by Marijohn Wilkin

I have returned to the Yahweh of Judah,

On my knees I did fall where the wall now stands;

This lesson I've learned as I've worked my way homeward,

The Savior of all is the comfort to man.

I have returned to the Father of Abraham,

The shepherd of Moses who called Him the great I Am;

He's Jesus to me, Eternal Deity;

Praise His name, I have returned.

DECREES

1. I decree a Holy Spirit outpouring is beginning to move upon all flesh, upon our sons and daughters.

2. I decree a billion soul harvest will be reaped as revivals spread across the land, pulling our prodigals back home to Father.

3. I decree revivals will occur in hundreds of places where our young people gather, in all 50 states and nations of the world.

4. I decree God is on our side, defending our cause and saving our children.

5. I decree God is pouring out His Spirit and changing things. He is avenging our children and healing their emotions.

6. I decree God is destroying the works of the forever loser. God is releasing His holy and good fathering anointing into the earth.

7. I decree our sons and daughters are discovering that Father loves them, wants them, and is preparing a place for them.

8. I decree that chains are falling off in Jesus's Name and truth is revealed—and the truth is setting them free.

9. I decree that I am taking the limits off of my thinking and know that You are able to do exceedingly, abundantly above all I could ever ask, think, or imagine.

10. I decree Romans 2:4 that God's kindness leads to repentance.

92

COME HOME

Jesus gave us the parable of the prodigal son to make this point—never mind what you've done, it's time to come home.

—Smith Wigglesworth

L et's take a closer look at what Jesus has to say about prodigals. There's nothing like what Jesus says. In Luke 15, the Pharisees had come to Jesus, complaining about with whom He had been associating, and even concerning with whom He was willing to eat dinner. After listening to their complaints, Jesus told them three parables.

A parable is often a true story that the rabbis used to adapt to their present times to illustrate a point. Or, it could be an apocryphal story they would use, taking a story from history and using it to make a point for the present. "Apocryphal" means of doubtful authenticity, although widely circulated as being true.

Jesus's first parable is called, "The Lost Sheep":

Suppose one of you had a hundred sheep and lost one. Wouldn't you leave the ninety-nine in the wilderness and go after the lost one until you found it? When found, you can be sure you would put it across your shoulders, rejoicing, and when you got home call in your friends and neighbors, saying, "Celebrate with me! I've found my lost sheep!" Count on it—there's more joy in heaven over one sinner's rescued life than over ninety-nine good people in no need of rescue.

(Luke 15:4-7 MSG)

95

If a shepherd has 100 sheep and one gets lost, he is going to go search for it. He will put the other 99 sheep in a safe place in a pen, and he will go out and find that lost sheep. A shepherd never gave up on a lost sheep; he was always on the lookout. That's the picture of Father's heart in our times right now, and Holy Spirit is amplifying it as we begin a very unique harvest season. Father is out looking for lost ones. He is seeking to find them and bring them back into the fold. He will not rest until He gets them back. He never gives up. He never stops reaching. He never stops trying.

The second parable is "The Lost Coin," and once again, Jesus's story concerns a search:

> *Or imagine a woman who has ten coins and loses one. Won't she light a lamp and scour the house, looking in every nook and cranny until she finds it? And when she finds it you can be sure she'll call her friends and neighbors: "Celebrate with me! I found my lost coin!" Count on it—that's the kind of party God's angels throw every time one lost soul turns to God.*
>
> **(Luke 15:8-10 MSG)**

In this parable, a widow searched until she found her lost coin. The coin was much too valuable for her to give up the search. She looked high, low, and everywhere until she found that lost piece of gold.

The third parable Jesus told is called "The Parable of the Prodigal Son":

> *Then he said, "There was once a man who had two sons. The younger said to his father, 'Father, I want*

right now what's coming to me.' So the father divided the property between them. It wasn't long before the younger son packed his bags and left for a distant country. There, undisciplined and dissipated, he wasted everything he had. After he had gone through all his money, there was a bad famine all through that country and he began to feel it. He signed on with a citizen there who assigned him to his fields to slop the pigs. He was so hungry he would have eaten the corn-cobs in the pig slop, but no one would give him any. That brought him to his senses. He said, 'All those farmhands working for my father sit down to three meals a day, and here I am starving to death. I'm going back to my father. I'll say to him, Father, I've sinned against God, I've sinned before you; I don't deserve to be called your son. Take me on as a hired hand.' He got right up and went home to his father. When he was still a long way off, his father saw him. His heart pounding, he ran out, embraced him, and kissed him. The son started his speech: 'Father, I've sinned against God, I've sinned before you; I don't deserve to be called your son ever again.' But the father wasn't listening. He was calling to the servants, 'Quick. Bring a clean set of clothes and dress him. Put the family ring on his finger and sandals on his feet. Then get a prize-winning heifer and roast it. We're going to feast! We're going to have a wonderful time! My son is here—given up for dead and now alive! Given up for lost and now found!' And they began to have a wonderful time."

(Luke 15:11-24 MSG)

There are King's kids scattered everywhere and the King wants them back. There are prodigal sons and daughters who have left Father's house, but He hasn't forgotten about them and He longs for them to return. He says, "Forget the law; I'm extending grace. Their sins are no match for My mercy. I want them back in My family. I want to restore them. I want their gifts and their talents. I want their abilities and purpose restored. I want them to have My name and reign with Me."

We cannot be like the older son and resent their return. Some of those who return are going to do far more than we ever thought about doing. They are so talented, so gifted. I am convinced that some of our greatest pastors, evangelists, prophets, and apostles are currently prodigals.

We must not think, *How can God restore and use some prodigal more than me? Who are they to be used in the Kingdom? They ought to be condemned and not celebrated.* Just be thankful your journey hasn't included four years of slopping hogs! You have been with the Father every day. You've been enjoying the palace. Your journey didn't take you away; you didn't experience that loss.

We must understand Father God's heart of unconditional love for us, and for them. We can't be jealous. We ought to celebrate along with the Father. We're all in the family. We are all heirs. All of us win. Who cares who gets credit? Let a prodigal hit the homerun that wins this thing! I just want a Kingdom win!

We are in a very special season whereby Holy Spirit is reaching out to prodigals. A supernatural blanket of conviction is going out into the world. Not condemnation—that's totally different. Conviction means the drawing power of God's love. It's a supernatural anointing that tugs at the heart and draws someone in. If God's lifted up, everyone is drawn in.

God is reaching out to prodigals. He has released angels of revival and angels of evangelism to reach them. It's the season for millions of prodigals to come home, and we are to be the ones who help them find their way. We're to reach out and help them return to Father's house.

Holy Spirit is emphasizing this parable of the Prodigal Son to the body of Christ right now. It's a special season for prodigals—lost sons and daughters—to come home. It's a Kingdom of God mission that has wind on it. It's time for the wandering kids to come back.

I believe the return of prodigals is the first phase of the harvest in this third great awakening that is now to be reaped. They are part of the Kingdom talent pool who will help our Kingdom reign with Christ. A blanket of conviction is going out and finding backsliders, those who used to worship and serve Christ, who used to rejoice together in God's house. Holy Spirit and His angels are actively ministering to find and restore them.

The prodigals are being wooed back to Father. That's part of conviction. Holy Spirit and His angels are busy waking up the prodigals and pressing them to come home. They are busy with dreams and connections. They are also wrestling, just as Jacob wrestled with God. Yes, there is a loving wrestling. God is going to lovingly wrestle for the destinies of prodigals.

Holy Spirit and His angels are throwing a net out to catch millions and millions of lost sons and daughters. The call of the Father is so clear. We are to partner with what Holy Spirit is doing. Partner with the new push. Pray it. Pray it. Pray it. That's our responsibility, partnering, praying and pushing in this present campaign.

God is calling us to embrace and accept the prodigals and backsliders. Restore them. Forgive and befriend them. We don't dare be self-righteous, religious Pharisees. It's time for prayer and intercession. It's time to begin to draw the prodigals back to Father's house.

Perhaps you are a prodigal and you need to come home. I have no doubt Holy Spirit is wooing you right now. Maybe there was a tragedy, a divorce, bankruptcy, or a death in the family that caused you to run. Perhaps it was a Pharisee who was judging you. Maybe ruinous living drew you away. Come home. Father wants you to reign with Him. He wants to restore you and make you an heir. Just talk to Him. He will run to you; He wants to embrace you. Won't you come home?

BILLY

One of the things that I enjoyed doing in my younger years was going deer hunting; and I would often stay with my grandparents during those times. It was something I could do to be with them, as I was rarely able to see them. So whenever I went deer hunting, that's where I would stay.

I remember one occasion when I was around 40 years old and my grandparents were getting up in age. After hunting all day, I was sitting and looking at my grandfather in his recliner and realized I really didn't know that much about him. I knew him as a grandpa, and he was a great one, but I didn't know a lot of details concerning his life. I think kids sometimes grow up knowing "that's grandma and that's grandpa," yet they don't really know their lives outside that parameter.

Anyway, it suddenly struck me that there were details of my grandpa's life that I was unaware of, so I began to ask him questions such as, "When did you see your first car?" He told me about how he had ridden a mule during most of his early life and what it was like when he saw his first car. Those were the kind of questions I asked him that evening.

Then I asked, "Grandpa, how did you come to know the Lord?" When I asked him that, my grandmother, who was sitting on the couch, said, "Tell him everything, Billy." So my grandpa began to share his salvation story with me.

He said, "Your grandmother received the Lord and would attend church regularly, but I would not." In his own words, he admitted, "I was a rascal and was certainly not following the Lord. But a revival came to the church and your grandmother went to it night after night, and she would ask me every day, 'Bill, will you go to the revival with me tonight?'" And he said that he would always say to her, "No, I'm not going."

Grandpa continued, "This went on for three or four days and she would ask me every day to go to the revival. Finally, I relented and said, 'Okay, I'll go.'"

Grandpa said they went to the revival and sat toward the back, and as he listened to the preaching, he said something began to happen inside him. He said, "I felt this draw toward the Lord," and he didn't really know how to describe it.

We would define it today as the convicting power of the Holy Spirit that manifests as a love that draws you to God. You know you're a sinner, you know you're wrong, and you know you need to receive Jesus.

I remember in some of the revival meetings when I was a kid, the convicting power and atmosphere of God's love would come into the room and draw people to where they would shake under that kind of power. They would grip the pews under conviction. They were being drawn as they heard, "You need Jesus, you need Jesus. You're guilty of sins."

My grandfather continued with his story, "I felt this overwhelming presence around me and I knew I needed to receive Jesus, but I resisted. We went home and I didn't say anything."

The next day, my grandmother said to him, "Bill, go to the revival with me again tonight."

But Grandpa said, "No, I'm not going."

She went out into the garden where he was and said again, "Please go to the revival with me tonight."

Once again, he answered, "No, I don't really want to go."

An hour or so later, Grandma asked, "Bill, would you please go to the revival with me tonight?"

And Grandpa said, "Okay, I'll go."

He said they went to the revival that night and sat about three rows from the back, on the aisle. The preacher preached, and Grandpa told me, "I don't know what he said, but at the end, he began to give an altar call, and I was so overwhelmed with the presence of the Lord, I began to tremble a little bit inside."

Grandpa continued, "I finally stepped out into the aisle and knelt on my knees. I was three rows from the back. As I knelt there on the floor, I began to weep and then I actually began to cry."

My grandmother said, "Tell him all of it, Billy."

He said, "Well, I began to crawl up that aisle. I crawled up to the front row, and I laid by the front row up toward the altar, and I began to pray and ask God to forgive me for things that I had done."

He didn't go into all of the details, but he said he repented of his sins and asked Jesus into his heart.

I finally asked, "Grandpa, why did you crawl all the way up the aisle and then stop at the first row?"

He said, "Son, I wasn't worthy to go up that close. I felt because of the way I had lived, I couldn't go up and kneel at that altar, so I decided I would just stay a few feet back." So that's what he did; he gave his heart to the Lord, and immediately he changed.

The little town we lived in noticed the change. My grandpa meant it; he had given his life to the Lord and he began to serve Him. He began to serve that Church of Christ and the Christian Union Church with Grandma. He became an elder and the church treasurer, and served in that capacity for almost 50 years.

CONVICTION

The convicting power of the Holy Spirit is real. When we pray and ask God to intervene in the lives of the unsaved or the prodigals, His love can begin to draw, convicting them of their sins. Yes, prodigals need to be convicted of their sins. And as my grandfather could testify, that convicting power of the Lord can draw you no matter if you're a rascal, no matter what has occurred in your life or what you have done. He can draw you to Himself.

My grandfather taught me how to love God. He taught me the love of a father. He was one of the most gentle, loving men that I have ever met. In many ways, I am in ministry today because of the ministry of a grandfather who loved me, who helped me get through Bible school, and enabled me to become who I am today.

The conviction of the Lord is a special love that reaches out and never gives up on anyone. It never gives up on a prodigal. It never gives up, no matter what they do, and will always lovingly draw them back to the presence of the Lord.

So, praying for conviction is something that I believe the church needs to do. A loving draw of Father for the prodigals to come home is needed. Pray this over your prodigals. Pray this for the lost and ask Holy Spirit to lovingly draw them, no matter where they are, no matter what they are involved in, no matter how dark their situations. God loves them and can draw them into Himself.

DECREES

1. I decree the miraculous is beginning to activate, producing healings, miracles, and our prodigals returning home.

2. I decree that Father is seeking and finding our lost ones and is bringing them back into the fold.

3. I decree that the heart of Father God is being revealed to our prodigals and drawing them back home.

4. I decree that Holy Spirit is reaching out to convict our prodigals with God's unconditional love.

5. I decree that backsliders who used to worship and serve Christ are being restored to Father's house.

6. I decree that Holy Spirit and His angels are waking up the prodigals and pressing them to come home.

7. I decree a hunger is developing in our prodigals for the presence of God.

8. I decree that God is visiting our prodigals in their dreams and reminding them of words that have been planted in them, and I decree those words will not return void.

9. I decree the everlasting faithfulness of God over our children.

10. I decree the enemy loses and God wins.

Come Home

by Rachel Shafer

(Spontaneous song of the Lord during a worship service)

Bring our sons and daughters home

Let them know Your great love

Bring them back to You

Back to the arms of the Father

Back to the house of the Father

Bring them back to You

There is no shame

There is no condemnation

Just love, just love

THE GOD HUG

THE GOD HUG

I want to share the parable of the prodigal son again, but from a different translation. There is something in the words Jesus used when He was telling this story that is found in the original language, the original Greek text. I feel very prompted to focus on this.

This story would affect His disciples from Pentecost through the rest of their entire ministry lives. My heart leapt inside me when I saw this. God's Word is so alive. Just one word can quicken things.

There is a wind of Holy Spirit on this amazing parable of the prodigal son as if it's being freshly told to us. It's prophesying, I believe, into our moment right now, a phase of our Kingdom's movement in this era. Jesus told His disciples:

> *A man had two sons. The younger son told his father, "I want my share of your estate now before you die." So his father agreed to divide his wealth between his sons.*
>
> *A few days later this younger son packed all his belongings and moved to a distant land, and there he wasted all his money in wild living. About the time his money ran out, a great famine swept over the land, and he began to starve. He persuaded a local farmer to hire him, and the man sent him into his fields to feed the pigs. The young man became so hungry that even the pods he was feeding the pigs looked good to him. But no one gave him anything.*
>
> *When he finally came to his senses, he said to himself, "At home even the hired servants have food enough to spare, and here I am dying of hunger! I*

will go home to my father and say, 'Father, I have sinned against both heaven and you, and I am no longer worthy of being called your son. Please take me on as a hired servant.'"

So he returned home to his father. And while he was still a long way off, his father saw him coming. Filled with love and compassion, he ran to his son, embraced him, and kissed him. His son said to him, "Father, I have sinned against both heaven and you, and I am no longer worthy of being called your son."

But his father said to the servants, "Quick! Bring the finest robe in the house and put it on him. Get a ring for his finger and sandals for his feet. And kill the calf we have been fattening. We must celebrate with a feast, for this son of mine was dead and has now returned to life. He was lost, but now he is found." So the party began.

Meanwhile, the older son was in the fields working. When he returned home, he heard music and dancing in the house, and he asked one of the servants what was going on. "Your brother is back,' he was told, 'and your father has killed the fattened calf. We are celebrating because of his safe return."

The older brother was angry and wouldn't go in. His father came out and begged him, but he replied, "All these years I've slaved for you and never once refused to do a single thing you told me to. And in all that time you never gave me even one young goat for a feast with my friends. Yet when this son of yours comes back after squandering your money on prostitutes, you celebrate by killing the fattened calf!"

His father said to him, "Look, dear son, you have always stayed by me, and everything I have is yours. We had to celebrate this happy day. For your brother was dead and has come back to life! He was lost, but now he is found!"

(Luke 15:11-32 NLT)

In this magnificent depiction of Father God's heart, Jesus tells us that when the father saw his lost son off in the distance, he ran to him. He didn't walk or stroll; he ran. The father was looking for his son to return. He was anticipating it and when he saw him, he ran to him. It's the only time Christ ever depicts Father God as running.

The great God of Heaven and earth is not depicted here as sitting on the throne of the universe ruling and reigning, though most certainly He does. He is not depicted as standing before billions of angels and giving them orders, though He does. He is not depicted as riding a chariot of fire as the most awesome conquering warrior in all of time and eternity, though He is. He is not depicted as the great I Am leading people in awesome deliverance and promised inheritance, though He is. He is portrayed as Father God, filled with unconditional love running to welcome a lost child home.

There could be no greater graphic portrayal than the one Jesus gives us here. Instead, religion and pharisaical ideas have portrayed Father God in a completely different way.

Religion says: "I messed up, my dad is going to kill me!"

Sonship says: "I messed up, I need to call my dad."

Jesus tells us as soon as He sees prodigals returning, He runs to welcome them, kissing their cheeks and hugging their necks.

GOD IS RUNNING

We are moving into an amazing era and this world is going to see Father God run. He's running with a divine purpose. He's going to run and He's going to bring the lost sons and daughters home. He's going to run and He's going to restore them. He's running to help them; He will clean them up and put new clothes on them. It is a present campaign being launched right now by Holy Spirit.

In Luke 15:20 (KJV), Jesus uses words that we need to focus on because it speaks to another awesome aspect of this campaign I believe is now beginning. He says in essence, "When the father saw his lost child coming, he ran to him and fell on his neck, kissing him."

"Fell on him" or "fell on his neck," as King James puts it, is the Greek word *epipipto* (Strong's 1968). It would ring in the hearts of these disciples for the rest of their lives. It would become a common phrase in the early church, throughout the book of Acts, and the apostolic travels in the New Testament. Its understanding gives such great hope. *Epipipto* means to embrace someone in love, to hug someone in love, or it means to hug someone you love. *Epipipto* was called the love embrace.

In Acts 10:44, Peter was at Cornelius's house. Remember, Cornelius was a Gentile. He was Italian. The Jews had no dealing with Gentiles. They were prejudiced against them because they were considered unclean people. They were from the other side of the tracks. You don't eat with them, you don't have anything to do with them, you certainly don't fellowship with them.

Holy Spirit gave the apostle Peter a vision where he saw a sheet come down out of Heaven with all sorts of "unclean" animals on it. Holy Spirit said, "Rise and eat." But Peter said, "I'm not going to do that, they are unclean." Then Holy Spirit said, "Don't you call common or unclean what I have cleaned." Through this vision and Holy Spirit's admonition, Peter then understood these people were not unclean. God can make them clean, and Peter began to minister to them. He obeyed the Word of the Lord and he began to declare the Gospel of Jesus Christ to the Italian people.

THE HOLY SPIRIT HUG

We are told that while Peter was declaring the Gospel to them, Holy Spirit fell on them and they spoke in other tongues. "Fell on them" is the word *epipipto*. Same word. While he was talking to them, God suddenly reached out in love and embraced these unclean people. While he talked to them and they received the Gospel of Jesus Christ, Holy Spirit hugged them. The love of God was poured out upon them. It was a baptism of love upon people who, up until that point, were considered to be unclean. Who, up until that point, had been treated as nobodies and low-lives.

Because of this outpouring, the entire direction of the early church (the Ekklesia) turned and Gentiles like us began to be welcomed into Christianity, which changed the course of history.

Peter said, "It has happened to them just like it happened to us," which was a reference to Pentecost. What happened at Pentecost to Peter and those who had gathered in the upper room had now happened to the people of the house of Cornelius.

On the day of Pentecost in Acts 2, many in that upper room were prodigals. Many of them who were seated in the upper room that day had forsaken Christ. They had turned their backs and walked away from Him at the cross. They went and hid themselves and some of them actually denied they even knew who He was. They disregarded His words; they were doubters. They had been with Him for three years, walking in His presence, hearing His words, but they took all of that for granted and walked away.

But on the day of Pentecost, they gathered together as a somewhat bedraggled house of faith. Some of them sitting there had messed up very badly. Some of them had missed God's plan by miles through unbelief. It was a mixed bag of men and women, young and old, sitting in that upper room. As they sat together in that room, they (in one accord) turned themselves toward God and suddenly there came a sound out of Heaven. It was the sound of Papa God leaving Heaven's porch to run to His children. It was the Holy Spirit coming in a baptism of Father's love. Holy Spirit fell on them (*epipipto*).

God, in the person of the Holy Spirit, hugged them and embraced them with unconditional love. He embraced them all, no matter what they had said, where they had run to, or how much they doubted. When they turned to Him, He hugged them. When they turned to seek Him, He fell on them with love. When they determined they were going to seek Him, the loving embrace of God's love baptized them.

What does the phrase "baptized in the Holy Spirit" mean? What does "outpouring" mean? Yes, it can mean an outpouring of power but here, Jesus gives us a different definition. What is a baptism of the Holy Spirit? It's when God hugs us with unconditional love. He baptizes us in His love.

In Acts 4:31 (KJV), we are told that God hugged them again, *"When they had prayed, the place was shaken where they were assembled together; and they were all filled* [again] *with Holy Ghost."*

They came to Him in prayer and He reached out and hugged them again. Ephesians 5:18 says we are to be filled and refilled with Holy Spirit. In other words, it's ongoing. You can fill up every day if you want to. You can come to Father every day for a fresh hug of His love. That's literally the definition.

UNCONDITIONAL LOVING EMBRACE

I sat by the lake a few years ago in the middle of the night, a place I go to often when I need to be alone and hear Father's voice. Carol and I were processing some things that had to do with transition. After months and months of walking through very difficult and dark times, and walking through a fierce time of spiritual warfare, stillness came and peace surrounded me. Understanding came and Holy Spirit fell upon me. Father God hugged me that night with His unconditional love. I felt His loving embrace and it changed everything. It gave me strength and confidence to move forward on a journey that He would take us on—one we're still on.

I knew we were to establish, with Holy Spirit's guidance and leadership, a Kingdom Ekklesia hub. I had no idea at that point what that really meant. I didn't know the journey ahead, but I knew in my spirit (in my knower) that this is what He was saying, and His loving embrace ministered to me that night.

A part of this campaign that is launching right now by Holy Spirit includes outpourings of Father God's love upon His people, and also upon those who are considered to be unclean people outside the fold. Baptisms of His love and power are now being poured out, not just on prodigals, but upon all His children, and whosoever will can receive salvation.

He's preparing to hug a billion souls right now. Think about it. We are moving into supernatural outpourings of Heaven whereby God hugs people. He hugs the lost. He hugs the family. He hugs them all, time and time again. An outpouring of Father's presence will now rise as never before and revival and transformation will surge.

There are so many today who need a God hug. They need to know that His arms do not reach out to push them away and never have. They certainly don't reach out to strike anyone. No, He runs to reach out His arms in love and hug them. His embrace changes everything.

THE OTHER PRODIGAL SON

The prodigal story tells us about two sons, not just one. There are those today who are like the first prodigal son, who have wandered from God's house and from His presence for various reasons. They need to be hugged by Father's love again. The good news is He will run with the opportunity to do exactly that. Let Him hug you and fill you with a baptism of His love and His presence. When His arms wrap around you, it changes everything.

There are also many who identify with the second prodigal son. Maybe you never left Father's house, but you haven't been entering in like you used to. Maybe you've been raised in church, possibly you've been around the presence of the Father all of your life like I have, but you're not really experiencing the joys of the household. You're physically there, but it's like you're standing outside.

Could there be some who have taken His goodness for granted? Who have forgotten about the abundant living that He provides us? Who have lost their first love, lost the joy, the first rush of what it was like to be a son or a daughter of God, and have forgotten that He's given an inheritance to all that He is?

Are there some in Father's house who once lived by the revelations of His Word that He gave to them, but now take those words for granted?

Are there some who are so used to Father's presence that it no longer impacts their actions?

To all of those who have wandered, Father God says, "What you need is another hug. One of My hugs will change this. What you need is another embrace." This is what I needed that night at the lake. "Come to Me and let Me baptize you in My love. Come and be filled by My Spirit again. Father says, let Me hug you. Let Me fill you again. Let My presence revive you. Let My anointing release you again. Let Me get close to you. Let Me talk to you. Let Me give you all I have. Let Me embrace you again in a baptism of My love. Let Me hug you with all that I really am."

You know what I think? Well, I'm going to tell you. I think the people of God need one of His hugs. Holy Spirit's campaign is launching to do exactly that, over and over and over again. Outpourings after outpourings. *Epipipto*. Embrace again, embrace again, embrace again. When you are in a spiritual battle, you need that embrace again.

We need to be baptized in His Spirit again. We need to be filled by His love again; and all we need to do to receive is turn to Him. What a concept! I wish I had been taught this when I was growing up. I was afraid of God. I was told, "If you do this or if you do that, you're probably going to hell." I never had a concept like this one—that any time I wanted, He would hug me. Just turn to Him and He will embrace me.

It's awesome to contemplate that the cure for prodigals isn't debasing penance. It's a hug from God, it changes everything. It is receiving His love embrace again. It's letting Him fill you with who He is.

The greatest days in church history are not in our past. They are in our present and our future and those days are now being launched, perhaps differently than you may have thought. "Oh," some say, "He's coming and He's going to clean house." Well, He may have to do that some, but Jesus says He is riding in to give people a hug. He's riding in to wrap His arms around a billion souls and say, "I love you. I'll change you. I don't care where you ran. I don't care what you did. I love you." And it will change everything.

You're going to see this outpouring revitalize the body of Christ in ways that we have longed for. Dead bones and dead hearts are coming to life.

Recently, at the Oasis where I am based, we have spent some time coming to the altars. We prayed for the prodigals, as well as other needs, but then the altars were open for God hugs. Could there be anything greater than that? I don't care what you are facing. I could tell the war stories, I have them. But I can tell you what a hug from God did. I still go back to that God hug. It changed everything, and He will do the same for you.

JIMMY'S STORY

When I was 7 or 8 years old, my dad was a traveling evangelist going from church to church. I was in meetings constantly as a young boy. One of the things that I learned concerning intercession for prodigals occurred when I was in one of those meetings.

At the end of the services, often the people of God would gather at the altars to pray for the lost. Back in those times, they didn't always refer to the altar as an altar, but would call it *the mourner's bench*. It was a place where people would allow the burden of the Lord to come upon them for the lost, and they would mourn in prayer for a lost loved one or for a lost friend, or it could have been a situation that they were mourning over.

As the burden of the Lord would come upon them, they would allow that burden to inspire their prayers. Often, as a child, I would see the saints gather to pray and intercede around those altars. This was a common occurrence, especially on Wednesday and Sunday nights at the end of the services.

One particular night, I saw a lady come weeping to the altar. She knelt and began to cry. I was only a few feet away from her and I was watching her intently because of how hard she was crying. She was sobbing, tears dripping down off of her chin.

Then she began to moan and cry over and over these words, *"God, don't let Jimmy go to hell. Jimmy's going to hell, God. Jimmy's going the wrong way. God, stop him. Don't let Jimmy go to hell."* The more she went on, the harder she wept and it got my attention. I had rarely seen someone cry that hard. I could tell her heart was broken.

Over and over, I don't know how many times, she kept saying, *"Don't let Jimmy go to hell."* I've never forgotten that intercession.

I asked my mom about this years later when I was older. "Do you know what happened to that woman's son?" I asked. Mom replied, "Oh yes, maybe three or four days later, he actually came to the service and your dad led him back to the Lord."

A prodigal was brought back home because of the prayers of a mother who went before God, carrying the burden for her son, and crying out to God. God moved on his behalf and brought him home.

The prayers of moms and dads, grandmothers and grandfathers, for their lost kids, their lost loved ones, are some of the most valuable prayers that can be prayed. It binds the work of darkness off their lives. Prayer breaks chains of bondage and sets them free. As in the case of the prodigal, it enables them to be enlightened and they come to themselves, thinking, *What am I doing?*

I don't know Jimmy's entire situation, but he came to himself and I have no doubt that his mother's prayers knocked the darkness off his eyes and he began to see his need to come back to the Lord, to return to Father's house. Never stop praying and being burdened for your children. Never stop talking to God concerning a lost child, friend, or loved one. Vital intercession is needed to bring the prodigals home.

It doesn't matter your situation. You may have drifted away and feel like you are the second son, on the outside looking in, not invited to the party. The Father simply says, "I'm glad you're back. All I want to do is restore you."

It's amazing that the great men who promoted the Ekklesia through all of the New Testament (Peter, Paul, James, John, and others) were included in another hug. Paul needed another hug. James needed another hug. Bartholomew needed another hug and God was there to give it.

Strength, encouragement, and enlightenment can come to you today.

Turn to Him today. No matter where you are in life, another hug is good.

DECREES

1. I decree Holy Spirit's presence is overwhelming me with His peace.

2. I decree there is a launch in the Spirit realm and things are shifting and an outpouring is manifesting.

3. I decree Father is running to help our sons and daughters come home. He is running to welcome them, to kiss their cheeks, and restore.

4. I declare a release of God's love on this generation, reclaiming and redeeming what the enemy has tried to lock up.

5. I decree God hugs released in this era to the prodigals, as well as those who have just grown weary or are not where they used to be.

6. I decree the steadfast love of the Lord never ceases and His mercies are new every morning.

7. I decree that as God's hugs are released that any bruises the enemy has tried to inflict are removed and healed—spirit, soul, and body.

8. I decree that the rich and pure love of God is reaching into our prodigals innermost beings and healing and restoring God's original intention for their lives.

9. I decree that God never ceases to gently and tenderly call my prodigal home.

10. I decree that one touch from the Father's hands changes everything.

CAST YOUR CARES

7

CAST YOUR
CARES

W e recently received the following in an email from an online member of Oasis who heard about the writing of this book:

I want to share what I know God is going to do in my family. It's too long of a story to explain the attacks and subsequent division, but three of our five children have walked away from the Lord or us or both. This messy story involves life difficulties mingled with lies and deception, leading to being duped by the enemy. We homeschooled our kids, prayed for them, and sought the Lord on their behalf, so they would have a foundation in Christ.

In spite of what we see and hear now, we KNOW our God will turn this for good just as He did for Joseph in Genesis 50 who said, "What you meant for harm, God has turned for good." This is actually a verse I have on my bathroom wall.

We will be like those who dream as it says in Psalm 126 (NLT):

When the Lord brought back his exiles to Jerusalem, it was like a dream! We were filled with laughter, and we sang for joy. And the other nations said, "What amazing things the Lord has done for them." Yes, the Lord has done amazing things for us! What joy! Restore our fortunes, Lord, as streams renew the desert. Those who plant in tears will harvest with shouts of joy. They weep as they go to plant their seed, but they sing as they return with the harvest.

My daughter wrote this years ago on a 3x5 card where it remains on our refrigerator as a constant reminder. And finally, Isaiah 58:12 that declares God will restore our homes. This is their inheritance and our children will turn back to the heart of our Father.

HE CARRIES ME

Holy Spirit has been speaking to me about some things and revealing truths to me concerning my belief and faith. Recently during my personal prayer time, I was praying about a particular issue that I have been praying about for quite a while now. And while I know that we are to keep praying and believing until we see breakthrough, I also know that we're not to be walking in worry. So while I may be praying for a certain thing, even for years, I can do that filled with faith and expectation.

But I found myself in a cycle of saying things like, "God, I'm giving this to You. I know it's in Your hands, You're working this for good." These are all things we know to believe and confess. But shortly after, I'd find myself dwelling on the issue again.

So I went to the Lord and asked, "Why do I keep thinking and worrying about this after I've prayed about it?" Right away, He said to me, "Because you keep taking it back." That is *not* what I was expecting to hear. He continued speaking to me and said, "You need to quit taking back the worry, quit taking back the burden." I didn't even realize that's what I had been doing, but it was exactly what I needed to hear, and I feel like this is a much needed reminder for all of us.

Casting

First Peter 5:7 (NKJV) says, *"Casting all your care upon Him, for He cares for you."*

The Voice Translation: *"Since God cares for you, let Him carry all your burdens and worries."*

J.B. Phillips Translation: *"So, humble yourselves under God's strong hand, and in his own good time he will lift you up. You can throw the whole weight of your anxieties upon him, for you are his personal concern."*

Let's look at the context of 1 Peter 5:7. The apostle Peter wrote this letter late in his life to encourage those facing persecution for their faith. The message he gives them is to stand firm on the Gospel and what Jesus has done for them. Following Jesus was becoming increasingly difficult and costly for the early church.

Peter was no stranger to the trials these Christians were facing. He himself had been flogged, beaten, and thrown in prison multiple times. He wrote from his personal experience to encourage them that God would come through, and He cared deeply for them. As he ends his letter, he gives his readers some words of encouragement as they are overwhelmed with the burdens of the world. I believe these words will be an encouragement.

Casting used in 1 Peter 5:7 is the Greek word *epiripto*, a compound of the words *epi* and *ripto* (Strong's 1968). The word *epi* means upon, as on top of something (Strong's 1909). The word *ripto* means to hurl, to throw, or to cast, and it often means to violently throw or to fling something with great force (Strong's 4496). The only other place this word *epiripto* is used in the New Testament is in Luke 19:35 (KJV), where the Bible says, *"And they brought him to Jesus: and they cast their garments upon the colt, and they set Jesus thereon."*

In 1 Peter 5:7, we see the idea of the word *epiripto*, which pictures the flinging of a garment, bag, or excess weight off the shoulders of a traveler and onto the back of some other beast, such as a donkey, camel, or horse.

We are not designed to carry the burden of worry, fretting, and anxiety. This verse is saying to take that load and heave it with all your might. Fling it over onto the back of Jesus and let Him carry it for you! Just as Luke 19:35 says they cast their garments upon the back of the donkey, now you need to cast your burdens over on the Lord and let Him carry those burdens for you.

As I was studying this, Holy Spirit reminded me of a dream I had many years ago. In the dream, God said to me, "Remember the first time I carried you." I remember weeping upon hearing those words in the dream. When I woke up, the dream was so vivid to me, as if I had audibly heard those words from the Lord. I began to try to figure out this dream and tried to remember when was the first time that Almighty God carried me.

During my prayer time, I started asking Him questions like, "Why do You want me to remember this? What are You trying to teach me?"

Moving

Many years ago, I went through a difficult time of infertility. I suffered multiple miscarriages and so, at the time of the dream, I thought back to my first miscarriage. That was the first time I really found myself in a situation of not knowing what to do, of wondering how something like that could be happening. It was the first time my faith had been tested in a very real, tangible way. I decided to look up the word *carry*.

Carry means to hold or support while moving. The image of being carried is that you're being held *while moving*. For example, if you are carrying your child, you are not standing still; that would be simply holding. Rather, you are moving your child somewhere. You may be carrying him because he's tired or to get somewhere quicker, or just to make things easier.

When God carried me through that first miscarriage, He carried me to a new place in Him. He moved me to a different level. When you pick someone up to carry them, you are bringing them higher. Higher levels give a different perspective. Think of a child who gets up on her dad's shoulders to see better, maybe to see above a crowd or to see a farther distance. It gives fresh perspective.

So when God carried me at this time, I began to see differently because I had His perspective. I became stronger and more trusting. I became more persistent. I became a fighter and more of a worshiper. It's easy to worship when life is good. It's much harder to worship when life is hard.

God had also told me in the dream to remember. *Remember* means to have in mind, or be able to bring to mind, an awareness of someone or something that one has seen, known or experienced in the past. It means to recall, recollect, or keep in mind.

So my question was why? Why did He want me to remember the first time He carried me? Then it dawned on me. He has *always* carried me. Sometimes He has had to rock and walk me gently while I wept in His arms. Sometimes He needed to carry me with a firm grip, so I wouldn't turn and run the other way. Sometimes He carried me when I didn't deserve it; He carried me just because He loves me.

Caring

Isaiah 46:4 (NLT) says in part, *"I made you, and I will care for you. I will carry you along and save you."*

The first time He carried me wasn't when I was going through my first trial. The first time He carried me was when I was born.

Isaiah 46:3 (NIV) says, *"Listen to me, you descendants of Jacob, all the remnant of the people of Israel, you whom I have upheld since your birth, and have carried you since you were born."*

There's never not been a day when He hasn't carried me. There's never not been a day when He hasn't carried my children and my family. And there's never not been a day when He hasn't carried you. I get weary in the waiting sometimes. I think that's when I have the tendency to take something back that I was never meant to hold. A worry or burden that I'm not supposed to carry. I'm supposed to cast it off and leave it with God. I constantly have to build up my faith by meditating on His Word and on His promises.

I believe the words I heard in my dream, "Remember the first time I carried you," was a way of reminding me that all my days and times are held by Him. From the time I was born—every moment—He knows the end from the beginning. And it was a powerful reminder that while I may think things are at a standstill, He is carrying me. It's what His Word says.

He is carrying my family, too, which means *He is holding us while moving.* I don't know what God is doing behind the scenes, but He has assured me things are moving. It is incredible to know you are in the powerful arms of Someone who loves you and cares for you.

The eternal God is your refuge, and underneath are the everlasting arms.

(Deuteronomy 33:27 NKJV)

He is carrying you and He is more than able to carry anything that concerns you. This includes any prodigals you may be praying for. The apostle Peter says we are to cast all of "our cares" upon Jesus.

The word *cares* is the Greek word *merimna*, which means anxiety (Strong's 3308). It is described as any affliction, difficulty, hardship, misfortune, trouble, or complicated circumstance that arises as a result of problems that develop in our lives. It could refer to problems that are financial, marital, job-related, family-related, business-oriented, relationships, sickness, or anything else that concerns us. It's all covered.

This means anything that causes you worry or anxiety *regardless of why it happened*. Certainly few things cause more anxiety, fear, or concern than when your loved ones are not following or serving Christ. This is what you need to throw over onto the shoulders of Jesus Christ! Nothing is too big or small to talk to the Lord about.

Peter says, because He "careth for you." The word *careth* is taken from the Greek word *melei,* which means to be concerned; to be thoughtful; to be interested; to be aware; to notice; or to give painful and meticulous attention (Strong's 3199).

Peter uses this word to assure us that Jesus really does care about us and the things that are heavy on our hearts. In fact, He gives meticulous attention to what is happening to us. He is interested in every facet of our lives.

In other words, when you put all these meanings together, 1 Peter 5:7 could read: *Take that heavy burden, difficulty, or challenge you are carrying—the one that has arisen due to circumstances that have created hardship and struggles in your life—and fling those worries and anxieties over onto the back of the Lord! Let Him carry them for you! The Lord is extremely interested in every facet of your life and is genuinely concerned about your welfare.*

PRAY TRUTH

You may be carrying a load or hanging onto a burden that isn't meant for you. Or you may be taking back what you say you're giving to God, like I was. You may say you're casting your cares, but they're still attached to you or you're reeling them back in.

So how do we truly cast our cares and leave them? I think the first answer is obvious:

1. *Pray...continually.* Prayer is how we can give our worries to God. Each one. We don't need to sugarcoat them or downplay our pain. We can simply tell God what we are feeling and worried about. We don't just pray once. We pray continually. First Thessalonians 5:16-17 (NLT) says, *"Always be joyful. Never stop praying."* Each time a worry comes up, we turn around and give it straight to God.

Another way to cast your cares is to:

2. *Remind yourself what's true.* When we face trials and challenges it's tempting to stop looking at and trusting God. We tend to focus instead on what's in front of us and the fear that is building. That's why it's so important to make it a regular practice to remind ourselves of the promises of God.

Replace your worry with the Word. Joshua 1:8 says to meditate on the Word day and night. Let me remind you of the reference in Chapter 4, *"I will save your children"* (Isaiah 49:24-25 NLT).

Philippians 4:8 (KJV) says, *"Finally, brethren, whatsoever things are true, whatsoever things are honest, whatsoever things are just, whatsoever things are pure, whatsoever things are lovely, whatsoever things are of good report; if there be any virtue, and if there be any praise, think on these things."*

Every time a situation arises, be armed and ready with a response from God's Word. God's Word always has an answer to any situation or problem. He will sustain you with peace that passes human understanding.

Turn over your worries and step into the life that He has for you. Turning to verses like 1 Peter 5:7 can be powerful reminders of what God has done and will do for us. In those moments we can remind ourselves: He is with me. He cares about me. He will sustain me. He loves me. He will carry me through this.

A third way to cast our cares:

3. *Take every thought captive. "We take captive every thought"* (2 Corinthians 10:5 NIV).

The Message version of 2 Corinthians 10:5 says: *"The world is unprincipled. It's dog-eat-dog out there! The world doesn't fight fair. But we don't live or fight our battles that way—never have and never will. The tools of our trade aren't for marketing or manipulation, but they are for demolishing that entire massively corrupt culture. We use our powerful God-tools for smashing warped philosophies, tearing down barriers erected against the truth of God, fitting every loose thought and emotion and impulse into the structure of life shaped by Christ. Our tools are ready at hand for clearing the ground of every obstruction and building lives of obedience into maturity."*

That is a loaded Scripture. The mind is where the battle between fear and faith takes place. Whatever you allow to captivate your mind will rule your life. So if you want the Word of God to reign over your thoughts, you have to resist the enemy when he tries to plant anything against it in your mind.

That's why, in order to cast your cares, you have to stop worried thoughts before they take root. You know how it begins. You hear something and a little doubt begins to creep in and your mind begins racing.

YOUR CHOICE

This is where you make a choice: Are you going to begin to worry or will you cast your cares? The only way to truly cast them is to take that thought captive immediately. Refute it with the Word of God. Declare, "I refuse to take this care or worry. I'm giving it to God because I know He cares for me."

Once you've taken a thought captive, if that worried thought tries to creep back in—pray. Decree God's Word. Don't give voice to the worry or fear. If you give worry a voice, you will create a place for it to live in your life. Instead, voice the Word of God. You'll find it is impossible to worry or be anxious when your spirit is in line with God's.

As I continued to meditate and study about how to truly cast my cares and when I had a good understanding of the spiritual principle and how to do that, Holy Spirit began showing me what I needed to take back. Things like hope, trust, faith, belief, joy, peace.

I hadn't fallen out of faith or belief, but I had grown weary. I was weary in standing and believing and in not seeing anything in the natural. The enemy wants to take things from you; we know he comes to kill, steal and destroy. We are not ignorant of his schemes and we don't have to allow it. If the enemy has succeeded for a time, it's time to fight back and take back. We see this principle over and over throughout the Bible.

In 1 Samuel chapters 29 and 30 we read part of the story of David:

> *And David was greatly distressed...but David encouraged himself in the Lord his God.*
>
> **(1 Samuel 30:6 KJV)**

This verse describes what had to have been one of the worst days of his life—and David went through some hard days and times.

In the context of this verse, David and his men had been away at battle when they returned home to Ziklag, and found that their enemies, the Amalekites, had taken *everything*. Their wives, children, and everyone else from their camp had been abducted. And to top it off—the Amalekites had burned the whole place to the ground.

Scriptures say that David and his men *"wept until they could weep no more"* (1 Samuel 30:4 NLT). Then it got worse. David's men were so bitter about what had happened, they began talking about stoning him! This is when David became greatly distressed and found himself at a crossroads.

CROSSROAD

But 1 Samuel 30:6 (NIV) says, *"But David found strength in the Lord his God."* *The Message* version says, *"David strengthened himself with trust in his God."*

Have you ever been at a crossroad like that? Maybe something bad has happened and you have a decision to make. Will you stay in the place of weeping, distress, worrying, doubting? Or will you stand up, fight, and take back what the devil has stolen from you? What we know is this—David recovered *all*.

So if we want to take back what the devil has stolen, we need to follow David's example. And the first thing he did was encourage himself in the Lord. That's not always the first thing that comes to our mind but it is a key to breakthrough.

How do you encourage yourself? First, with the Word of God like we've already talked about. Dive into the Word and remind yourself of what He has said about you, the authority He's given you, and the promises He has made to you. It is very hard to spend time in the Word and not walk away encouraged.

Second, remind yourself of all the victories He's given you. Remember those times He's healed you, delivered you, favored you, and defended you. Remembering builds your faith to where you'll be ready to run after the enemy and take back everything that's been stolen from you. David strengthened *himself* in the Lord his God and gained strength for determination to take back what the enemy had stolen. Remind yourself Jesus took back the authority from satan and gave the authority back to us as believers. We have a covenantal right to make a claim on these promises for our prodigals.

First Samuel 30:8 (NKJV) says, *"So David inquired of the Lord, saying, 'Shall I pursue this troop? Shall I overtake them?' And He answered him, 'Pursue, for you shall surely overtake them and without fail recover all.'"*

God gave David something *to do* (pursue). Then, God gave David a *promise* in the doing: *"You shall surely overtake them and without fail recover all."*

When God gives us something to *do*, He also gives us a *promise* in the doing.

First Samuel 30:18-20 (NLT) says:

> *David got back everything the Amalekites had taken, and he rescued his two wives. Nothing was missing: small or great, son or daughter, nor anything else that had been taken. David brought everything back. He also recovered all the flocks and herds, and his men drove them ahead of the other livestock. "This plunder belongs to David!" they said.*

David fought and took back his wives, children, and animals from the enemy. Everything that the enemy took, David took back. God gave him a complete victory and His promise was proved true.

DOERS OF GOD'S WORD

The promise was fulfilled completely, but it wasn't fulfilled as David just sat back passively, saying, "All right God, now You can do it." The Lord fulfilled His promise, but He used David's *actions* to fulfill the promise. In this time and season, we are called to be doers of the Word.

God's promise didn't *exclude* David's cooperation, the promise *invited* his cooperation. And because David engaged and partnered with God, God gave David *even more* than what He promised. He received spoil from the battle beyond what was taken from Ziklag. This was a blessing straight from the grace of God.

David strengthened himself in the Lord his God. He inquired of the Lord, believed God's promise, and did what God told him to do. Because of that, he was able to step into a time of restoration and redemption, taking back all and then some.

It is time to take some things back by the authority of King Jesus. I believe God is going to restore some things in your life, just as He did for David. What we're to do is cast our cares and worries, strengthen ourselves in the Lord our God and decree His Word. Confess that there will be nothing missing or broken and get ready for it!

JOB'S LOSS AND RESTORATION

In looking at another example in the Bible, it didn't look like Job would recover either. In the book of Job, we see that this upright and holy man of God was living in total misery. He didn't do anything wrong and yet he suffered a great deal.

One moment, Job was a picture of wealth, health, and happiness. The next moment, death hit and Job mourned the loss of seven sons and three daughters. Lack hit and all of his wealth disappeared. Sickness hit and there were open sores all over his body. Relationship troubles hit and his wife turned on him, telling Job to curse God and die. Even his once loyal friends lost respect for Job and began blaming him for his trials.

Can you imagine how alone, desperate, and defeated Job felt? He was being hit from every angle, with no sign of relief in sight. But in due time, God intervened. In Job 42:10, we learn that the Lord not only restored Job, but He gave him twice as much as he had before. He regained everything the devil had stolen and then some, double to be exact.

Today, we still serve the God of the double portion. The God of restoration and better than before. So when you go to reclaim and take back what the devil has stolen, don't just go for what you lost. Expect more. Know that God is turning things around in your favor. Your circumstances won't define what is going on in your life, God will.

TAKE BACK

After experiencing five miscarriages and all the loss and emotions of going through that, there were a lot of things the enemy was trying to take from me: my joy, my hope, my belief, my trust, my song, my peace. The enemy was trying to replace them with doubt, worry, unbelief, and fear. But those things couldn't define my heart when I spent time with Jesus and handed them back to the Helper.

When I gave God my worry, anxiety, and grief, He began to give things back to me. He said, "Here's your joy, take it back." God takes what was meant for evil and turns it for good.

Confusion couldn't define my heart when I would run my confusion to the Counselor, and He actually counseled me on what He sees, and what is to come. He gave me His perspective. He said, "You see the way that I see; take back your eyes of understanding."

Fear couldn't define my heart when I took that fear to the Comforter, and He said, "I've not given you the spirit of fear, but of power, love, and a sound mind—take back your peace," and He comforted me into peace with His promises. I had so much promise there was no room for fear.

When worry tries to creep into my heart, I take a few moments to get away and the Lord says: "Worry does not have to define your heart. Cast your cares on Me because I care for you." Take back your faith.

What are some things you may need to take back? Fill your mind with what His Word says, with what is true and authentic. Spend time with Him consistently, pray, read His Word, worship Him, pursue His presence. If you're feeling discouraged and disheartened, it's probably time to check in with God and take back what was stolen. Sometimes it's as simple as saying "Jesus" and letting His presence soak down into your spirit.

I am a testimony of His grace, mercy, and faithfulness—as someone who has learned to take life's situations and say:

- I know what it looks like, **But God**!

- I know there doesn't seem to be a way, **But God** will make a way!

- I know you may feel discouraged, **But God** is at work in your life!

We may feel weak, *But God* makes us strong. We may be in a storm, *But God* causes us to rise above. You may feel broken, *But God* makes us new and beautiful. You may be sick in spirit, soul, or body, *But God* is your Healer. You may be clothed in garments of loss, hope deferred, a spirit of heaviness, you may be weary, *But God*.

You may be distraught over days, weeks, months, even years of praying for your prodigal, *But God* sent His Son to, *"Console those who mourn...to give them beauty for ashes, the oil of joy for mourning, the garment of praise for the spirit of heaviness, that they may be called trees of righteousness, the planting of the Lord, that He may be glorified"* (Isaiah 61:3 NKJV).

It doesn't matter what the enemy has done, or tried to do, or will try to do, we know what we are called and purposed to do as the heirs of Christ. God knows the plans He has for you and they're good with a future filled with hope. God is still well able to fulfill the promises He has for you. Let your heart be defined by what *He* says.

PROPHETIC WORD

While studying and praying the Lord gave me this prophetic word, saying:

> *"I will restore the years the locust has eaten. The enemy who has taken advantage of God's people will be removed. I will give back harvests that have been destroyed. Your fields will yield an abundance that will make up for what has been lost. The threshing floor shall be full of grain and your vat will overflow with wine and oil. I am restoring all and I am restoring more. You are going to take back in double portions.*
>
> *"I am turning your mourning into joy and more joy. I am giving beauty and more beauty for your ashes. I am restoring your health to better than it was. Your*

fear is being turned to faith and that much greater faith. I am restoring more than was lost. Instead of shame and dishonor, you will enjoy a double share of honor. You will possess a double portion of prosperity in your land, and everlasting joy will be yours. Double downpours, double outpourings, double is now coming to you.

"What is seemingly impossible in the natural will be suddenly possible by My Spirit. Your intercession and worship has produced an atmosphere for breakthrough. Your breakthroughs are being prepared even now, says the Lord.

"I will give you strategies and My voice will open ways for you to do things in this season that will be accelerated. Once again I am going to dry up the sea by the wind of My Spirit and you will cross over into new territory and your enemies will drown in the returning waters. You are stepping into a season planned by Me and there will be shouts of praise as miracles and victory begin to break out one after the other. Don't be afraid, be glad and rejoice for I am now doing great and mighty things, says the Lord."

Those are some amazing promises to believe God for. Be assured of this: God's Word will come to pass in your life and He will restore. Even when it may not be well with our circumstances, it can be well with our soul. It's time to march into the enemy's camp and take back what was stolen. Take back what was taken in our personal lives, our children's lives, in our families, in our churches, in this nation and across this land. Believe God for greater, abundant, double.

DECREES

1. I decree Your faithfulness and I thank You for the promise that we can cast our cares on You because You care for us.

2. I decree a double portion of blessing and inheritance over every area of our lives.

3. I decree that You, God, will restore the years that the locust has eaten.

4. I decree breakthrough over my prodigal's life.

5. I decree that I will fight back, take back, and recover all.

6. I decree that hope and expectation will rise in my heart as I believe for my prodigal to come home.

7. I decree You are turning my mourning into joy.

8. I decree what is seemingly impossible in the natural will be suddenly possible by Your Spirit.

9. I decree You are restoring lost harvest and my prodigal is returning to You.

10. I decree I am taking back my trust and hope. I believe You are making things beautiful in my prodigal's life.

8

I AM REMEMBERING YOU

8

I AM
REMEMBERING
YOU

On March 14, 2023, Holy Spirit gave me a dream. In this dream, I saw long lines of prodigals—millions of them— walking over hills and mountains, beside and across rivers, and through downtown streets. I perceived that they were coming from everywhere on their journey, returning to Father God.

In these long lines of returning prodigals, I did not recognize the vast majority of them, but every fiftieth one or so, there would be a person who looked familiar. I might not have known the individual by name, but I knew he or she was well known, or even famous, for one reason or another.

As I began to notice these particular prodigals in the dream, I started picking up on their spheres of influence. For example, several were notable in the area of politics, government, or science, while others were prominent in media, education, or business. Or perhaps they were well known in the entertainment world, through movies or television.

As I paid attention to these particular prodigals, Holy Spirit anointed me to understand that they had once been taught concerning the love of Father God. They understood Christ's sacrifice for their sins. They had learned in Sunday school, church, or in some other way, to live according to Christian values, but had wandered away from God. Now, though, they felt a conviction to come back to faith. Father was reaching out to hug them, wooing them back to Him through His unconditional love.

Then—and this was a bit unusual, but it's a dream and they often are odd or strange—I was allowed to discern these prodigals' thoughts. For example, I heard:

- I can't stand this anymore; things have gone too far.
- Everything's crazy; this world is crazy.

- I don't believe what I'm being told I must believe.

- I don't want to say what they're telling me I must say.

- I don't believe men can have babies. I don't believe women can become men.

- I don't like the gender confusion that's being promoted and pushed upon our children.

- I don't believe abortion is right.

- I don't believe there are many ways to God. I believe there's only one way and it's through Jesus.

After hearing these thoughts, I then heard a statement. I don't know if it was Holy Spirit who said it, or if it was an angel, but I heard: *"They are returning to the Father and will now become His Kingdom's activists."*

In this dream, I was somehow made aware these prodigals would be like Saul of Tarsus in the New Testament. Saul was an activist working against Jesus, who hated Christians and made every effort to harm them. He obtained legal permission to falsely imprison Christians, even having some of them killed. We know that Saul was involved in the murder of one of the deacons in the first New Testament church, a man named Stephen (Acts 7:54–8:1).

Although Saul had been raised to live by God's Word, pharisaical religion had blinded him, and he diligently worked for hell's kingdom in order to destroy the efforts of the first Ekklesia. But one day as he traveled on the road to Damascus to persecute more Christians, Saul had an encounter with Jesus. A bright light came out of Heaven and knocked him right off of his donkey. I want to see that instant replay someday! When Saul hit the

I AM REMEMBERING YOU

ground, he heard a voice telling him, "I'm Jesus...the One you are persecuting!" (see Acts 9:1-6).

Long story short, Saul the activist repented. He sought forgiveness for his self-righteous rebellion and Father God hugged him. God fell on Saul with the baptism of the Holy Spirit and he became the apostle Paul, activist for the Kingdom of God, voice for the cause of Christ (Acts 9:10-20).

I heard, in this Holy Spirit dream:

> *"Well-known activists for hell's kingdom, who have been blinded by satan's deception, are having encounters with Christ Jesus. In some cases, they are being reached in dramatic ways, and everyone will hear about it. They are being confronted by Christ and they'll repent, becoming activists for His Kingdom. They are publicly going to switch sides. Some who have been well known in political realms, business, education, and media, and have carried an activist agenda, standing for doctrines of devils through their influential platforms, are coming to their senses. They are saying, 'This is crazy. This isn't right. I don't believe this. I can't do this anymore. I need to return to the God of my childhood.'"*

They are going to become bold activists for King Jesus declaring, "I am a Christian and God's Word says this is wrong; therefore, I will not support this." They will declare, "God's ways are best." They are going to become visible ambassadors for the Kingdom of Christ Jesus. There will be men and women in all the mountains of the culture of society becoming activists for King Jesus!

Something incredible is launching. Supernatural encounters with Jesus the King are accelerating and prodigals are returning home. People are coming back—those whom you or I may have a hard time believing that they would ever do so, just as the early church had a hard time believing the same about Saul. In fact, only one of the apostles even believed that he would turn. James, John, and Peter didn't believe it; they actually thought Saul was setting a trap for them. It was not until Barnabas went to see Saul in person, interviewed him, and then hand-led him to the Jerusalem church, saying, "I can verify that the anointing of the Lord is upon him and he's one of us," did they believe.

There are champions of hell that are going to be encountered by Jesus, who are going to return to Father, and we're going to exclaim, "She?" "He?" "They returned?!" And these former activists for satan are going to boldly represent the cause of Christ.

In the midst of an onslaught of demonic activity, it is of paramount importance that we hear what Heaven has to say! I was recently given this prophetic word: *"Those born from the womb of My intercessors will leap into their destiny callings. They will be forerunners who run, pointing the way to Jesus. They will be a different breed, converging with other remnant warrior generations to change history and present Christ the Messiah."*

GOD REMEMBERS

First Corinthians 2 talks about God revealing His secrets to us. Recently as I sat on our back deck pondering God's secrets, I said to Holy Spirit, "What is a profound reality Father God is saying for our times right now? What is a deep secret inside of the heart of

King Jesus or the Father that we should now understand and be experiencing?"

Immediately, without any delay or interlude, Holy Spirit said, "Father said, 'I am remembering you.'" It took me by surprise. I was not expecting that. I went into the house and told Carol, "I just heard God say, 'I'm remembering you.'" She said, "What does that mean?" And I said, "I don't know, but I'm going to find out!"

I heard Holy Spirit say, "Father said, 'I'm remembering My sons. I'm remembering My daughters.'" Something amazing is unveiling on this planet. It's never been seen quite like this before. God is remembering us in this era. I want you to get this: God is remembering *you*.

He said, "I am remembering My words to you. I'm remembering you." I instantly knew that the *you* was not just *me*. It was me and I needed to hear that, but I knew this was a different level. It was meant for the Ekklesia. It was meant for the remnant.

I knew I was to proclaim this as an apostolic prophetic word into this era that would activate some things. It was a word to His sons and daughters. It was a word to prodigal sons and daughters as well. He is remembering them.

I knew that had a meaning that I needed to look into because this was not a surface statement. What does the Scripture mean when it says, "And God remembered"? Of course He did. God doesn't forget. He forgets nothing, so this isn't the obvious He stated here.

The Hebrew word for *remember* is *zakar* (Strong's 2142) and it has a nuance that we need to understand and is so good to know. *Zakar* means to bring someone, or several someones, to mind and then act on their behalf. *Zakar* is not a mental act of remembering something. It is a direct action that is the result of remembering.

In the Scriptures that talk about God remembering someone, each one always includes God's actions on that person's behalf.

The following are biblical examples:

In Genesis 8 we are told that God remembered Noah and his family. That doesn't mean that God had forgotten about them. It's not like God was walking around Heaven and thought, *We have some guys and gals and animals in a boat down there.* No, it's the word *zakar.* God remembers and brings forth His actions to act on their behalf. He sent a wind that caused the flood waters to recede and dry land to appear.

In His remembrance, there was the supernatural release of His actions. In His remembering was a supernatural response. This always happens when the Bible says God remembers.

In Genesis 30:22, we are told that God remembered Rachel, Jacob's wife. She was barren and desperately wanted a child. She had cried out to God, time after time, crying out for years to have a child. One day the time came that intersected with a God-planned moment. We are told God remembered Rachel. *Zakar* is the word. What was the God action? He opened her womb. She was able to conceive, barrenness was broken, and Joseph was born.

In Exodus 2:24, we are told of God's people in Egyptian bondage. They were persecuted, enslaved, and under oppressive laws, rules, and task masters. But the Scripture says God remembered His covenant to Abraham, Isaac, and Jacob.

Again, of course God did! He forgets nothing. But the word is *zakar*—He brought it to mind with action. God sent Moses and He set them free. God destroyed Pharaoh's army. He gave them great wealth. There was a transfer of wealth. God healed each one of them. None of them left Egypt feeble. They were all healed. God took them to a land of milk and honey. He turned despair to gladness. In God's remembrance was and is His action, which is supernaturally activated in His remembrance.

Theologians tell us the phrase "God remembers" is an anthropomorphism. Never thought I'd use such a big word, did you? It is a figure of speech in which a finite human trait is ascribed to an infinitely powerful God so that we can understand Him more. Please understand when God remembers, it is always followed by proof He never forgets. Always. It has never not happened. It's proof He is acting on your behalf.

In Acts 10:31, an angel of the Lord appeared to Cornelius and said, "God has heard your prayer." And he said, "God has remembered your alms, your giving to the poor." In that remembering was God's actions. He sent the apostle Peter to him to preach the Gospel of the Kingdom and Cornelius gathered his whole household together, their extended family, and Peter preached the Gospel to them—and we are told that his entire household was saved. In the remembering were God's actions. In the remembering was God's response. In the remembering was God's deliverance. In the remembering was God's great salvation.

We have entered into an era like the children of Israel in the Exodus did, like Noah, Rachel, and David who cried out, "God, remember me," and God did. God surrounded David with mercy and lovingkindness and delivered him from his enemies.

Father said, "I'm remembering My Word to My people. I'm remembering My word to the Ekklesia." Meaning, prophesying, My action on their behalf has been released. It's now in process. I'm remembering My prophetic words to you and My supernatural action on your behalf is activating to deliver you and set you free.

I'm remembering and acting on your behalf. Proof of it is manifesting. Barrenness will break. Flood waters will recede. Storms will be calmed. Deliverance is activating. Enemies are going to be drowned. Hamans are going to hang. New territories are opening. Covenant promises are flowing. Prodigals are coming home.

Father says, "I'm remembering words I spoke to you ages ago. I'm remembering words I spoke to you in your youth. I forget nothing. *Zakar.* My actions on your behalf have now begun. I will save your children. I will save your households. I will provide. I will heal. I will free you."

Psalm 145:4 (MSG) makes the powerful statement that each generation tells stories of God's mighty acts. While previous generations have seen amazing moves of God, the current and coming generations have only seen glimpses. However, I believe this is about to change. Holy Spirit gave me a word concerning this that is now coming into its moment.

Holy Spirit said:

> *"Doors to new history will soon open. A new movement will soon spring forth. A new stream from My throne is now flowing, a pure stream of powerful Gospel. It will be preached by all generations, races, colors, and ethnicities. For the stream of My Gospel has been diverted and dammed up by those who wanted the benefits of 'reservoired' blessings; but I will now blow up the dams, says the Lord. The religious dams, the cultural dams, and racial dams. I will discipline the spiritual hoarders. I will discipline the dividers. I will have the Gospel that flows freely with My Spirit.*
>
> *"My movement will move. It is built to move and it will move, empowered by fresh wind and soaked with fresh oil. My Kingdom's river will flow without dams.*

Downpours of glory rains will fill it to overflowing and it will leap to flood stage. For I have prepared a pure Gospel voice, a glorious Ekklesia, lit with the fires of My cause; one that I can confirm with signs, with wonders, and with miracles; one that is not diluted with flesh, pride, immorality, racism, or greed; one that I can back with awesome Kingdom assets; one that I can marshal Heaven's army behind. A Gospel of awesome power will now surge forward and the generations will synergize their efforts for the revival of ingathering.

"I am calling to My Gideons: 'Come from your hiding places. Come from the ghettos. Come from the mountains. Come from the plains. Come from the projects. Come from the country. Come from the city and stop the raiding of My harvests. Yes, I have seen you, says the Lord, behind the winepress. I have seen your secret toil and I have heard your cry for relief. Now hear My cry. Now hear My voice. Rise and see the strong arm of the Lord. Now see My plans change your future. Yes, I have seen your heart and I will empower you. You will defeat the enemy, and you will enjoy the spoils of victory.' And you will say, 'Our enemy has resourced us. Our enemy has stored abundance for us. We have more because of war.' Yes, dams are breaking and blessings, deliverance, and inheritance will flow.

"For a shift in leadership will soon come, says the Lord. A new breed of leaders will be revealed in My Kingdom. The obscure ones who have served faithfully will now receive promotion. Though man has

not seen, I have seen, says the Lord, and it will be said, 'Where did they come from? Who are they?'

"And I will advocate for them, says the Lord. I will say, 'These are they who have come from My presence. These are they who would not compromise. They would not be muzzled. They would not bow to darkness. These are they who would not appease humanity with enticing words but have stood strong for My words.'

"They did not flinch. They did not bend their knee to blended religion and doctrines of devils or doctrines of men. They did not tolerate the diluting of My message and the mocking of My ways. They have stood unashamed for Me; now I will stand unashamed for them. I will side with them, says the Lord. I have proclaimed their victory and I will oversee its completion.

"Multiplied graces will now flow. Bound souls will be set free. Captives in heart will be delivered. Those blinded by sin will be liberated from hell's bondage as the revival of ingathering leaps forward.

"My Kingdom generations, in sync with My angel armies and soaked in the fresh rains of Heaven, will now leap forward into great revival. They will move in power, passion, and purity, and I will back them with manifestations of My mightiness. Notable miracles will leap forth. Notable victories will leap forth in their midst.

"For the revival in the womb of My intercessors is now leaping forth. The revival birthed in the womb of those in travail will now be proclaimed in the earth. It is time for the forerunners to run into destiny *callings, declaring, 'Jesus is the way, He is the truth and He is the life.'"*

The closest friend of Jesus was John the Baptist, who was called a forerunner. As a young man around 30 years of age, he ministered a message that pointed to Jesus as the Way, the Messiah and the Savior. You may remember that when John was just a babe in his mother's womb, he leapt at the sound of Mary, Christ's mother.

In reference to the coming generation in this era, Holy Spirit said to me, *"Those born from the womb of My intercessors will leap into their destiny callings. They will be forerunners who run, pointing the way to Jesus. They will be a different breed, converging with other remnant warrior generations to change history and present Christ the Messiah."*

Recently, I attended my granddaughter's college graduation at Lee University. The commencement ceremony was held outside in a large area surrounded by beautiful buildings. As I looked around during the reading of the names and giving of the diplomas, I noticed I could see Stone Chapel. This was one of the places, along with many other college campuses, where revival occurred for several weeks this past winter. Thousands of lives were touched by this outpouring of the Holy Spirit.

As I was pondering and reflecting, watching young men and women in their caps and gowns, waiting for their names to be called, I heard Holy Spirit say, *"Look at how many I have hidden behind the winepress."* I knew exactly what He meant. Holy Spirit was referencing when Gideon hid behind a winepress to thresh wheat because the Midianite armies were stealing Israel's harvest. Gideon was hiding in fear when his name was called.

He was called out of that time of fear and vulnerability, to stop the raiding of Israel's harvest. Gideon answered the call and he, along with his 300 remnant warriors, stopped the raiding, routed the enemy, and restored the lost harvest.

Holy Spirit then said:

> *"I am calling their names. They will run with Me, pointing the way to Jesus. They will rout the enemies and stop the raiding, working alongside other generations. I am now calling out the names of young men and women of valor: 'Come run with Me. Graduate into your place in the generations.' I will call out the names of multiplied thousands of Gideons. They will hear Me call their names, for I know their names. The raiding and stealing of harvest will stop and the reaping of harvest will begin. History will be changed."*

When God calls your name, He is calling out your identity and purpose. He sees past any natural limitations and calls forth your destiny.

What an amazing era is unfolding. A new breed of leaders is being revealed in God's Kingdom. We must pray for this coming generation who are called to be forerunners. Many of them are now prodigals but their names are being called by the Father. We must mentor, assist, promote, support, and run with them. We most certainly were born for such a time as this.

> *"Pray for your children. Wrestle with God for them night and day."*
>
> **—Charles Spurgeon**

DECREES

1. I decree God is remembering me and is acting on my behalf.

2. I decree we have entered into an amazing era and are seeing God move supernaturally in every realm to accomplish His purpose.

3. I decree God is remembering the prodigals in my life and is drawing them home.

4. I declare He is releasing His power to change, create, save, redeem, and restore everything He has spoken to me.

5. I decree an acceleration of this word to bring these promises forward in my life.

6. I decree prodigals in different spheres of influence are returning to Father God.

7. I decree those who have known or served God in the past, but have wandered away, are being wooed back to Him.

8. I decree prodigals are coming to their senses, realizing they have been lied to by the enemy, and are returning home.

9. I decree well-known individuals are going to have encounters with Jesus and will be bold activists for His cause.

10. I decree supernatural encounters with King Jesus are accelerating and prodigals are returning home.

I remain confident of this: I will see the goodness of the Lord in the land of the living. Wait for the Lord; be strong and take heart and wait for the Lord.

—Psalm 27:13-14 NIV

ABOUT THE AUTHORS

TIM SHEETS

Dr. Tim Sheets is an apostle, pastor, and author based in southwestern Ohio. He ministers nationally and internationally at conferences, churches, seminars, and Bible schools. He is a graduate of Christ for the Nations Institute and has a Doctorate of Divinity from Christian Life School of Theology.

He is the author of: *Angel Armies; Angel Armies on Assignment; Planting the Heavens; Heaven Made Real; The New Era of Glory; Ninjas with Feathers; Prayers and Decrees That Activate Angel Armies;* as well as *Come Home* and *God's Got This,* both coauthored with his daughter, Rachel Shafer.

Dr. Sheets is the founder of AwakeningNow Prayer Network and the pastor of Oasis Church in Middletown, Ohio.

Dr. Sheets resides with his wife, Carol, in Lebanon, Ohio. They have two children, Rachel (Mark) Shafer, and Joshua (Jessica) Sheets, and 7 grandchildren (Madeline, Lily, Jude, Jaidin, Joelle, Sam, and Grace).

Tim Sheets Ministries
6927 Lefferson Road
Middletown, OH 45044
TimSheets.org
Phone: 513-424-7150

RACHEL SHAFER

Rachel Shafer is an author, worship leader, songwriter, and speaker. She ministers regularly at church services and conferences. Her book *Expect God* answers the question of what to do when your problem is hiding your promise. Her message is one of deep faith, abiding hope, and expectation in life's unexpected moments. In her book *God's Got This,* she teamed up with her father, Tim Sheets, to provide a powerful resource for parents and children filled with devotions and biblical decrees to speak over every season of life.

Rachel is the worship leader at Oasis Church in Middletown, Ohio, and has released many recording projects with Oasis Worship including "I'll Be the One," "God of Breakthrough," "War Cry", and "A New Day." She also released "America's Anthem," a song filled with prayers and decrees over our nation.

Rachel resides in Ohio with her husband, Mark, and their four children, Madeline, Lily, Jude, and Jaidin.

Rachel is available to minister for weekly services, conferences, and gatherings of all types. She has been interviewed on podcasts, TV stations, and radio. To contact Rachel, visit Rachel Shafer Ministries at rachelshafer.com.

From
Tim Sheets

Activate Heaven's angel armies to move on your behalf!

When you decree and declare what the Bible says, the angels of God are activated to perform the works and wonders of the Lord on your behalf.

In this powerful book, Dr. Tim Sheets draws inspiration from his bestselling *Angel Armies* series to offer Spirit-empowered decrees that bring Heaven to earth. You will be equipped to speak words that mobilize the heavenly hosts to accomplish God's victorious plan for your life.

As you use these prayers and declarations, your words will release the power to:

· Cut off the strategies of hell and bring transformation and deliverance to entire regions.
· War victoriously in the spirit realm as angels give assistance and provide protection.
· Mobilize the hosts of Heaven to unlock miracles, signs, and wonders.
· Plant the Heavens" with words, decrees, and prayers that release biblical results.
· Unlock the Third Great Awakening.

Multitudes of angels have been waiting for you to release them on assignment with bold, Scripture-saturated decrees. Open your mouth, speak God's Word, and watch the angel armies bring Kingdom transformation to your world!

Purchase your copy wherever books are sold.

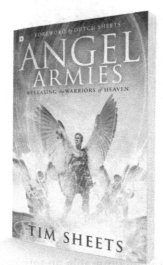

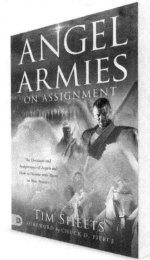

From
Tim Sheets

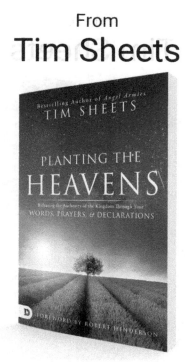

Pray the Prayers that God Wants to Answer!

The words we speak in prayer are like spiritual seeds. In the same way that planting seeds in the ground produces a harvest, you can learn to pray in a way that plants the blessings of heaven here on Earth.

Tim Sheets shares a revelatory new message that will take your prayer life to powerful new dimensions. Grasp the impact of your declarations and discover the power of praying the words that Heaven longs to hear!

Get ready to:

- **Pray with authority:** learn how your prayers and proclamations are supernatural forces in the unseen realm
- **Pray with confidence:** bring your words into agreement with God
- **Pray with expectation:** partner with Heaven to transform your life, family, church and region for the Kingdom of God.

Learn how to activate God's timeless strategy for victory, blessing, and revival by planting the Heavens with seeds of prayer!

Purchase your copy wherever books are sold.

From
Tim Sheets

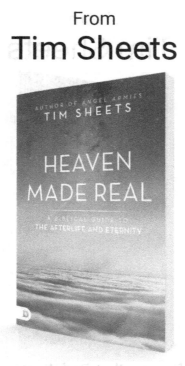

The Best Is Yet to Come

Heaven is real—even more real than this physical earth! Heaven is so much more than a "parallel universe" or a place we go after our time on earth is done. Plants, animals, and people live there! Heaven also has a position and a dimension! For all those curious questions you've ever asked, *Heaven Made Real* has answers.

In these pages you will find Biblical truths and answers to some common questions many Christians face in their journeys with God:

- What does Heaven look like?
- Where is Heaven located?
- What will our bodies look like in Heaven?
- How will we live?

Whether you're an avid believer or a seeker of truth, you'll see Heaven in a whole different light. It will change your life!

Purchase your copy wherever books are sold.

From
Rachel Shafer

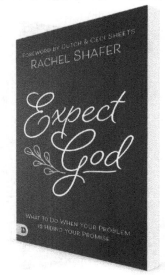

What are you *expecting?*

Life is filled with unexpected journeys, both good and bad. While it's often easy to see God in the good times, it can be challenging to hold onto hope in the midst of tragedy and impossibilities. In the darkness, things often seem hopeless.

But what if God could introduce unexpected, supernatural solutions? What if the giants you are facing didn't have the final word? What if something impossible and irreversible could be changed miraculously?

Wife, mother, and minister Rachel Shafer takes you on a raw journey through her compelling story, filled with angelic intervention, Holy Spirit revelation, divine dreams, and supernatural encounters.

From five miscarriages, to adopting a child with special needs, to a cease-less onslaught of medical issues, Rachel learned in the darkness how to expect God to come through—and He did, again and again!

When you expect a God-encounter in your darkest hour, He will redeem what seems hopeless with supernatural answers!

Purchase your copy wherever books are sold.

From
Tim Sheets & Rachel Shafer

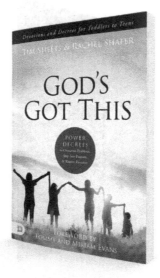

Powerful Decrees to Equip All Ages for Spiritual Victory!

There is a war against your children. Every day, kids of all ages are bombarded with the enemy's lies that war against their God-given identities and divine destinies.

But when kids speak God's truth over themselves, their minds are renewed and they become rooted in a healthy, Bible-based identity.

In *God's Got This*, notable apostolic leader and prophet, Tim Sheets teams up with his daughter, author, speaker, and worship leader, Rachel Shafer to provide a powerful resource for parents and children—biblical decrees that kids can speak over themselves in every season of life.

Don't let the world control your children! Equip them with powerful declarations to stand against the enemy's lies and walk in the truth of their divine identity!

Purchase your copy wherever books are sold.

From
Tim Sheets & JD Hornbacher

What would you do if you met your Guardian Angel?

That's exactly what happens when Zoe asks for God's help to deal with the school bully, Talia. But Zoe gets more than she expected when her angel, Joph, takes her on an incredible mission to battle the demon, Fearmonger. On this assignment, she must gather the pieces of the Armor of God so she can remove the fear-seeds planted by Fearmonger.

But can she face her hidden fears and greatest mistakes? Can she trust God and make the ultimate choice to bring freedom to herself, her loved ones, and even her worst enemy?

This hilarious and impactful story will answer tough questions about God, while empowering you to live with strength and confidence. On this exciting journey, you will discover how partnering with God's angel army can bring victory to your life and Kingdom transformation to the world around you!

"What did you think angels did?" Joph asked.
"I don't know," I admitted. "Like, sit on clouds and play harps all day."
Joph rolled his eyes. "Well, I do play a mean harp, but no. We are defending you, secretly and unseen, fighting against evil forces."
I scrunched my nose in confusion. "When? How? I never see any of that happen1"
"I know." Joph struck a karate pose. "We're like ninjas. With feathers."

Purchase your copy wherever books are sold

YOUR Prophetic COMMUNITY

Sign up for a **FREE** subscription to the Destiny Image digital magazine and get awesome content delivered directly to your inbox!

destinyimage.com/signup

Sign up for Cutting-Edge Messages that Supernaturally Empower You

• Gain valuable insights and guidance based on biblical principles
• Deepen your faith and understanding of God's plan for your life
• Receive regular updates and prophetic messages
• Connect with a community of believers who share your values and beliefs

Experience Fresh Video Content that Reveals Your Prophetic Inheritance

• Receive prophetic messages and insights
• Connect with a powerful tool for spiritual growth and development
• Stay connected and inspired on your faith journey

Listen to Powerful Podcasts that Propel You into God's Presence Every Day

• Deepen your understanding of God's prophetic assignment
• Experience God's revival power throughout your day
• Learn how to grow spiritually in your walk with God

In the Right Hands, This Book Will Change Lives!

Most of the people who need this message will not be looking for this book. To change their lives, you need to **put a copy of this book in their hands.**

Our ministry is constantly seeking methods to find the people who need this anointed message to change their lives. **Will you help us reach these people?**

Extend this ministry by sowing three, five, ten, or *even more* books today and change people's lives for the better! Your generosity will be part of catalyzing the Great Awakening that many have been prophesying and praying for.